The Healing Power of
Sleep

Mary O'Brien, M.D.

Biomed General
Concord, California
© 2009

The Healing Power of Sleep

P.O. Box 5727
Concord, CA 94524-0727
USA

925-288-3500 (tel)
925-680-1201 (fax)
info@biocorp.com

Author
Mary O'Brien, M.D.

Editors
Holly Stevens
Richard S. Colman, Ph.D.

Cover Design
Rex Salazar

Illustrations and Layout
Erika Paras-Salinas
Megan O'Keefe

ISBN 978-1-893549-17-3

This book is not designed to substitute for professional medical advice. Always consult a medical professional before making major changes in eating habits or taking supplements.

To obtain more information about Biomed General's products and services, please contact us at the above address.

About The Author

Dr. Mary O'Brien (M.D.) is board-certified in internal medicine and geriatrics and has served on the medical school faculties of Georgetown University and the University of North Carolina. She is also a board-certified Physician Nutrition Specialist. She frequently lectures to health professionals on neurology, women's health issues, pharmacology, and nutrition.

About
Biomed General

Biomed General is an organization that provides health care professionals with the latest scientific and clinical information. Biomed's live seminars and home–study courses are designed to help health professionals provide better care for their patients. Biomed General operates nationwide in the United States as well as internationally.

Biomed General
P.O. Box 5727
Concord, CA 94524-0727
USA

925-288-3500 (tel)
925-680-1201 (fax)
info@biocorp.com

Dedication

This book is dedicated
to my father,
who has always been
able to sleep like a log,
and to my mother,
who wishes that she could.

Dr. Mary O'Brien

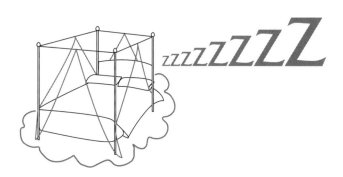

Table of Contents

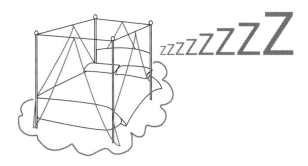

Preface

Sleep is one of the most vital yet incompletely understood human functions. It's usually not a serious problem when we're little kids or teenagers, but by the time we approach mid-life, sleep, or lack thereof, can become an absolute nightmare (sorry, couldn't resist that one). The surprising part is how little time and attention is devoted to sleep problems in everyday clinical medicine. There is a number of excellent sleep disorder clinics across the country, but in reality, only a small number of people has access to them. Most primary care doctors are extremely busy handling acutely and chronically ill patients, mountains of paperwork, and endless bureaucratic battles. Taking a detailed sleep history often becomes lost in the shuffle. If a patient does complain of insomnia, she might receive some cursory advice on over-the-counter sleep aids or perhaps a hastily scribbled prescription for 10 Ambien (zolpidem) caplets. Unfortunately, neither of those options will truly address the problem long-term.

I'm embarrassed to admit how inadequate my own medical training was on the entire subject of sleep. We were always much more focused on "real" problems like heart disease, diabetes, hypertension, and cancer. Only recently have we started to realize that sleep deprivation can exacerbate all of those life-threatening conditions. I always thought it ironic (okay, idiotic) that we tormented the sickest patients in the hospital by waking them up every 10 minutes to check their vital signs. The sicker someone is, the more she needs sleep. There's a happy balance for almost everything in life, even in the intensive care unit. But in the course of our love affair with technology over the last 30 years, we've fallen way off balance. If we really want people to recover from a significant illness or trauma, we must preserve and protect sleep.

I learned this lesson the hard way. Getting a good night's sleep was simply not a problem for me as a teenager.

Then I went to medical school. Nothing has been the same since. Night after night of being on call takes its toll. After a while you begin to anticipate being awakened. Then you begin to dread it. Next thing you know you can't relax enough to fall asleep in the first place. I could single-handedly raise insomnia to an Olympic caliber event – 9.8 on technical skill – I didn't even flirt with Stage 2 sleep! (Stage 2 sleep will be outlined subsequently.)

Have you ever noticed that when you have a problem or condition, you tend to read everything you can on the subject? You think about it. You study it. You develop greater understanding and empathy for others with the same problem. Hence, this book. My intention is to bridge the gap between the sleep medicine textbooks (yawn) and the superficial information found in magazines. If you're a nurse or a pharmacist or a social worker or therapist of some sort, perhaps you'll be able to pass this information on to your patients. Even critically-ill patients feel better after a good night's sleep. That means there's hope for the rest of us.

Chapter 1

What is Sleep Really?

"Blessings light on him who first invented sleep! – it covers a man all over, body and mind, like a cloak; it is meat to the hungry, drink to the thirsty, heat to the cold, and cold to the hot; it is the coin that can purchase all things; the balance that makes the shepherd equal with the king, the fool with the wise man."

—Miguel de Cervantes Saavedra, *Don Quixote* (1605 - 1615)

Understanding Sleep Structure

Experts in the field have defined sleep as a reversible, behavioral state. Well, isn't that helpful! I suppose that would help distinguish sleep from coma, which is not easily reversible. We know we feel dreadful when we don't get enough sleep. We know sleep is not merely a passive state. On the contrary, sleep is a highly active process regulated by the central nervous system. It involves or affects every organ system of the body.

With any luck, one-third of our life is spent sleeping, and the remaining two-thirds is profoundly influenced by the quality and quantity of our sleep. Even one night of inadequate sleep can ruin our mood, impair our judgment, and sour our interactions with everyone else. Virtually all of us can relate to this based on personal experience. But a good understanding of sleep architecture is essential to helping patients.

Sleep is far more than the absence of wakefulness. It's usually a complex physiologic, psychological, and behavioral condition coordinated by neurons and neurotransmitters in the brain. There are two distinct types of sleep – rapid eye movement (REM) sleep and non-rapid eye movement

(NREM) sleep. NREM sleep includes Stages 1 through 4. (These stages are explained below.) Then REM sleep or dream sleep occurs. It takes approximately 90 minutes for an adult to pass through all five stages of sleep.[2] This is known as a sleep cycle. A baby's sleep cycle takes about 60 minutes.

Each stage in a sleep cycle has distinct characteristics and a specific electroencephalogram (EEG) pattern. During wakefulness, the EEG reveals rhythmic alpha waves at 8 to 12 cycles per second (cps).[2,3] As we make the transition from being awake to being asleep, we enter Stage 1 sleep. Alpha waves begin to fade, and low voltage theta waves predominate at three to seven cps.[2,3] Stage 1 sleep is very shallow or light sleep. It is fragmented sleep, and we are easily awakened at this point. Our eyes move very slowly, and there is little muscle activity. Stage 1 sleep is not refreshing or restorative at all.

Stage 2 sleep is the longest stage of sleep. New waveforms appear on the EEG. These are known as sleep spindles and K complexes.[2,3] During Stage 2 sleep, eye movements ease, but you may still wake

> Stage 1 sleep is very shallow or light sleep.

up fairly easily. Older adults and many people with chronic illnesses can spend most of the night in Stage 2 sleep. It's better than being awake, but it's certainly not the most restorative or refreshing sleep.

Stages 3 and 4 are sometimes referred to as priority sleep. These are deeper stages of sleep associated with delta or slow-waves on the EEG.[2,3] During deep or delta wave sleep, it's difficult to wake up. And when you do, chances are you feel dazed and disoriented. Many of our body's repair processes occur during slow-wave sleep. Muscles, bones, and joints heal assorted injuries and micro-traumas. Skin and other connective tissues regenerate or repair themselves largely during Stage 3 sleep. During Stage 4 sleep, the anterior lobe of the pituitary gland synthesizes between 70% and 80% of our total daily allotment of growth hormone. Growth hormone is important for achieving normal adult height, but it also helps us maintain normal muscle mass, strength, endurance, and stamina. Without adequate levels of growth hormone you feel like a dish rag! Growth hormone levels fade considerably as we age, and in many chronic illnesses. This is one of the reasons it's virtually impossible to feel well if we're sleep-deprived.

Many neurotransmitters are synthesized in Stage 4 sleep, including acetylcholine, critical for memory and learning, dopamine, vital for staying focused and alert, and serotonin and norepinephrine, essential for well-being. No wonder sleep deprivation feels so miserable. When we spend inadequate amounts of time in deep, slow-wave sleep, we deprive our brain of what it needs to produce normal levels of hormones and neurotransmitters.

The final stage is known as REM (rapid eye movement) sleep. This is when most dreaming occurs and body functions accelerate. In REM sleep, breathing becomes more shallow, irregular, and rapid.[2,3] Eyes move in a jerking manner in various directions, but there is muscular paralysis in the extremities. This prevents us from acting out dangerous dreams. During REM sleep, we see a rise in the pulse and blood pressure. There is an increase in oxygen consumption, and blood flow to the brain increases.

Perhaps you've had the experience of waking up

abruptly when the alarm clock rings and feeling as if you were in the middle of a dream. Chances are you were. We tend to spend longer periods in REM or dream sleep as morning approaches.

In the last few years, research has demonstrated that REM sleep is far more important than previously recognized. It enables us to consolidate memories (never pull an "all-nighter" before an exam!) and enhances creativity and daytime efficiency. The more intense or complicated your job is, the more you must preserve and protect REM sleep.

The Importance of Sleep-Wake Cycles

Sleep and wakefulness are controlled by two key processes. One is known as circadian process, and the other is homeostatic process. Circadian, or daily rhythms, are thought to be regulated by an internal biological clock that runs in 25-hour cycles. This influences our need to fall asleep, wake up, or doze off in the afternoon. This "master-clock" appears to be in an area of the brain called the suprachiasmatic nucleus, just above the optic chiasm (crossover point of the optic nerves just in front of the pituitary gland). Circadian rhythms have tremendous influence on functional ability or impairment. A good example is the pattern of single-vehicle car accidents. The greatest number of these accidents occurs between 2:00 am and 6:00 am and also between 2:00 pm and 4:00 pm. These represent the two sleepiness peaks in our biological rhythm.

The homeostatic process is not completely understood, but it seems to rely on a variety of chemicals that accumulate almost like a "sleepiness factor" while we're awake. Some of these chemicals include GABA (gamma-aminobutyric acid), melatonin, galanin, and adenosine. GABA is an inhibitory neurotransmitter that keeps too many stimuli from activating the brain. Melatonin and galanin are hormones that facilitate sleep, and adenosine is a chemical modulator that is antagonized or blocked by caffeine. These substances tend to concentrate in a region of the brain called the ventrolateral preoptic nucleus (VLPO).

The awake state is influenced by histamine in an area of the brain known as the tabero-mammillary nucleus (TMN).

Current theory proposes that balance between the VLPO and the TMN determines sleep or wakefulness. A number of other neurotransmitters gets in on the wakefulness gig, including acetylcholine, serotonin, and norepinephrine.

But wait! There's more. Exposure to light has a major effect on sleep-wake cycles in general, and the master-clock, or suprachiasmatic nucleus (SCN), in particular. Sunlight sends a message to the suprachiasmatic nucleus that it's morning and time to get in gear. This helps us to reset circadian rhythm for the next 24 to 25 hours.[4] That's nice. Here's what it really means—when insomnia strikes, the worst thing we can do is to sleep in late. Wrong message to the SCN! We need to get up at our usual time and get some bright sunlight (if there is any).

> When insomnia strikes, the worst thing we can do is to sleep in late.

How Much Sleep Do We Really Need?

More than what we're getting! It seems to me almost everyone is tired all the time. Before the invention of the light bulb, the average American slept nearly 10 hours a night. There's only so much you can do by candlelight. In 1910, average nightly sleep was in the nine-hour range, and by 2002, it had fallen to the seven-hour range. The fact is, millions of people try to get by night after night on five or six hours of sleep. Then we wonder why we feel so awful. There's no mystery here.

Over the last few years, we've had no shortage of polls and studies on this subject. And statistics can be very helpful at times. But I can't ignore what I've learned hanging out in hospitals over the last 30-some years. We live in a society that views fatigue as a sign of weakness. It's especially trying in medical circles (and, I would imagine, in the military). Medicine is full of machismo. We were expected to work 120 hours per week without whining. Working 36 or 40 hours without sleep was standard operating procedure. Unfortunately, it didn't make us more sensitive or understanding of the needs we all have for rest. In fact, we used to brag about how little sleep we had gotten. Perhaps you can relate. But human physiology hasn't changed simply because we have electricity. Human beings still need seven to eight hours of sleep each night. Of course, virtually everything in medicine involves a bell-shaped curve. A few folks can do fairly well with less sleep, and there are those who generally need more. But most of us fall in the middle. And let's not forget the kids. Little ones typically need 10 to 11 hours of sleep every night, and teenagers do well with about nine hours. Oops. No wonder we see so much crankiness and bad behavior. It's amazing how many problems would be solved if we'd just go to bed when our mothers told us to.

Here are a few tips that will tell if you're getting enough sleep:

★ Can you wake up most mornings – when you need to – without an alarm clock?

★ Can you get through most days without feeling drowsy?

★ Can you read a newspaper or sit through a lecture without dozing off?

★ Can you go through the day without being irritable or distracted?

The Effect of Aging on Sleep

Well, for starters, it's not good. Most of us have heard the myth that older people simply don't need as much sleep. Not so, according to researchers working with the National Sleep Foundation. Older adults need as much sleep as anyone else, they just don't get it all at once. As we age, sleep becomes more fragmented. In fact, both subjective and polysomnography determined that sleep deteriorates with advancing age.[5,6] And we're not talking about centenarians here. Noticeable changes in sleep occur in our 30s and it's downhill from there, or as the academicians phrase it, sleep "worsens progressively through at least the eighth decade."[7]

Here's a list of what we can look forward to:

★ Delayed sleep onset – it takes longer to fall asleep.

★ Increased wakefulness after sleep onset – you wake up a lot during the night.

★ Reduced perceived depth of sleep – you're not sure you really slept at all some nights.

★ Decreased sleep efficiency – you spend more time in bed – wide-awake.

★ Decreased percentage of slow-wave or deep sleep (if you get any at all).

★ Increased percentage of Stage 1 or light sleep.

Doesn't that sound swell? And we haven't even gotten to a discussion of medical disorders yet! That's OK. You can't understand pathology until you understand physiology. And clearly, the physiologic changes of aging explain a lot, when it comes to sleep.

A Word About Women

If you thought the physiologic changes of aging were depressing, wait until you hear about the joys of being female:

★ Approximately 80% of women report premenstrual symptoms that include insomnia.[8] Sleep is most disturbed during the two or three nights before menstruation begins – estradiol levels are at their lowest, and fatigue and assorted discomforts are increasing. The time of the month you need sleep most is when you're least likely to get it.

★ About two-thirds of perimenopausal women have difficulty sleeping.[9] As menopause approaches it takes longer to fall asleep (sleep latency increases), sleep is more fragmented by frequent awakening, and a corresponding increase in daytime-fatigue occurs.

★ In the first trimester of pregnancy, there is an increase in total sleep time and more daytime sleepiness. By the third trimester, total sleep time decreases, and there are many more nocturnal awakenings courtesy of various aches and pains, nausea, heartburn, nocturia, and fetal movements.

★ Pregnant women may also experience more snoring, sleep disordered breathing, and problems with restless leg syndrome (often because of iron deficiency).[10]

★ New mothers experience legendary sleep deprivation just keeping up with the baby's sleep and feeding schedule. Who got up in the middle of the night to take care of a fussy baby at your house?

★ During menopause, many women struggle with delayed sleep onset and frequent awakenings, some of which are caused by hot flashes, sometimes as often as every 8 to 10 minutes through the night! That'll make you cranky.

Well, so far we've defined the terms relating to sleep architecture and identified some of the neurotransmitters and hormones involved in the process. We've established average sleep requirements and the particular effects of age and hormonal fluctuations in women. That covers the bases in terms of basic physiology. Now we're poised to discuss the next step – the consequences of sleep deprivation.

References

1. Carskadon MA, Dement WC. Normal human sleep: an overview. In: Kryger MH, Roth T, Dement WC, eds. *Principles and Practice of Sleep Medicine*. 4th ed. Philadelphia: WB Saunders Co; 2005: 12-23.

2. Kruger, MH, Roth T, Dement WC, eds. *Principles and Practice of Sleep Medicine*. 4th ed. Philadelphia: Saunders: 2005.

3. Kelly DO. In Kandel ER, Schwartz JH, Jessell TM, eds. *Principles of Neural Science*. 3rd ed. New York: Appleton and Large; 1995: 792-804.

4. Piggins, HD. Human clock genes. *Ann Med.* 2002; 34: 394-400.

5. McCall WV. Management of primary care sleep disorders among elderly persons. *Psychiatric Serv.* 1995; 46 (1): 49-55.

6. Prinz PN, Vitiello MV, Raskind MA, et al. Geriatrics: sleep disorders and aging. *N Eng J Med.* 1990; 323 (8): 520-526.

7. Hirshkowitz M, Moore CA, Hamilton CR 3rd et al. Polysomnography of adults and elderly: sleep architecture, fragmentation and leg movement. *J Clin Neurophysio* 1992; 9(1): 56-62.

8. Mamber R, Bootzin RR: Sleep and the menstrual cycle. *Health Psychol* 1997 May; 16(3) 209-214.

9. Miller E. Sleep Disorders and Women: Women and insomnia. *Clin Cornerstone* 2004; 6 Suppl 1B: 58-18.

10. Moline M, Brach L and Zak R. Sleep Problems Across the Life Cycle in Women. *Curr Treat Opt Neurol.* 2004; 6: 319-330.

Chapter 2

Physiologic Consequences of Sleep Deprivation

"That we are not much sicker and much madder than we are is due exclusively to that most blessed and blessing of all natural graces, sleep."

—Aldous Huxley
Themes and Variations on a Philosopher (1950)

Do you remember the last time you worked all day, then stayed up half the night working, or caring for a sick child or spouse, and still had to work the next day? Didn't you feel more than mere fatigue? Perhaps you had a headache, sore muscles, queasiness, achy (burning) eyes, a scratchy throat, or chills. You almost feel as if you're fighting a virus. If you're a mom, or you've ever had to be on-call overnight, you probably know exactly what I'm talking about. And that's just after one rough night. It's disconcerting to think about the consequences of chronic sleep deprivation, but we need to do precisely that if we're going to prevent any of them.

The Tired Heart: Too Pooped to Pump

You can't do much reading in this field without encountering the work of Dr. William Dement, one of the world's most prominent sleep researchers and co-founder of the Stanford University Sleep Disorder Clinic. In his book, *The Promise of Sleep*, Dr. Dement makes a very bold statement, "There is plenty of compelling evidence supporting the argument that sleep is the most important predictor of how long you will live, perhaps more important than whether you smoke, exercise, or have high blood pressure or cholesterol levels.[1]" I'm not sure I buy the part about smoking, but apart from that I think he may be right.

> Sleep is a critical time enabling the body to heal, repair, restore, and regenerate itself.

Sleep is a critical time enabling the body to heal, repair, restore, and regenerate itself. When sleep is compromised, restorative processes seem to be hampered. Fluctuations in blood pressure, catecholamine production (adrenaline), and hormone synthesis appear to be exacerbated, impeding our ability to bounce back. Over extended periods, these disruptions of normal function may well push a vulnerable organ system over the edge to disease.

A number of studies conducted over the last few years confirms a link between obstructive sleep apnea and the risk of transient ischemic attack (TIA), stroke, atrial fibrillation (A-fib), recurrence of A-fib after cardioversion (electric shock to restore normal rhythm), and sudden cardiac death. [2,3,5] The damage engendered by sleep apnea seems to be cumulative and the mechanism of action is probably related to the one-two punch of inflammation and elevated blood pressure. [4]

Sleep apnea is certainly a serious condition, and we'll discuss it in greater detail later, but simple sleep deprivation can wreak havoc with heart function. The Harvard Nurses' Health Study has looked at the sleeping habits and cardiac problems of nearly 70,000 women over a 10-year period. The study's findings rang some alarm bells. Women who consistently slept only six hours each night had an 18% greater risk for myocardial infarction (MI) than women who usually slept eight hours. Women who slept nine or more hours per night were also at increased cardiac risk.

If you recall what happens in rapid eye movement (REM) sleep, for example, a possible explanation emerges. During REM sleep blood pressure and pulse rate increase. And, just before awakening, the stress hormones adrenaline and cortisol surge into the bloodstream. If someone already had another risk factor for heart disease, say hypertension, elevated lipids, or smoking, the resulting stress on the heart could be even more severe, especially if they are sleep-deprived. If the heart is pushed to work harder – beating faster, raising blood pressure, and constricting arteries – an MI or stroke could occur. Isn't it interesting that one of the most common symptoms of an MI in women is unusually pronounced fatigue for the month prior to the event?

If you're much over the age of 30, you may have experienced a more common effect of fatigue on the heart – skipped beats. Premature atrial contractions (PAC's) and premature ventricular contractions (PVC's) are usually not serious, but they surely can be disconcerting. You may notice your heart skipping beats when you lie down at the end of the day. If you're slender, it may feel as if your heart is slamming up against your sternum, not painful, but definitely unpleasant. Too much caffeine can certainly exacerbate the situation as can adrenaline pumping in response to stress. I've never even had a cup of coffee, but I've had prolonged periods of ventricular bigeminy (skipping every other beat) and even ventricular tachycardia (V-tach) after several bad nights on-call.

A little low dose beta-blocker can help settle things down, but the best remedy is regular, sound sleep.

Sleep Deprivation & the Endocrine System

I doubt you'll read this statement in any textbook, but once someone develops an endocrine problem, chances are good another one will crop up at some point. At times, it seems as if there's almost a domino effect. A perfect example would be Polycystic Ovary Syndrome. The problem often begins in the ovaries, but eventually the patient may develop obesity, hyperglycemia, insulin resistance, hypothyroidism, and adrenal gland dysfunction. Medically speaking, it's a mess.

In Chapter One, we mentioned a vital relationship between Stage 4 deep sleep and growth hormone synthesis. An ever-increasing body of research is revealing a connection between sleep deprivation and obesity, and most of it seems to be modulated by hormonal disruptions.[6]

Researchers at Eastern Virginia Medical School in Norfolk looked at 1,001 patients from several primary care practices. They measured body mass index (BMI) and sleep habits and found a fascinating link: Overweight patients reported about 1.8 hours a week less sleep than the normal weight patients. That doesn't prove a cause-and-effect relationship, but it certainly merits attention.

> Overweight patients reported about 1.8 hours a week less sleep

The ongoing Wisconsin Sleep Cohort Study, begun in 1989, has provided additional insights along the same line. They looked at sleep duration, BMI, and early morning hormone levels in 1,024 people. Those who slept less had lower levels of leptin, a hormone that acts on the hypothalamus to suppress appetite. Less leptin often translates into more eating. "Short sleepers" also had higher ghrelin levels. Ghrelin is a hormone produced by the stomach when it's empty. It stimulates the hypothalamus to increase appetite. The bottom line – BMI was inversely proportional to sleep duration. Or in normal-person English, the less people slept, the more they weighed.

A much smaller study conducted at the University of Chicago looked at circulating leptin and ghrelin levels in 12 healthy men in their 20s. When the men were allowed only four hours sleep, they had 18% lower leptin levels and 28% higher ghrelin levels. They were also more hungry and craved carbohydrates like cookies, candy, and cake. Now I understand why cookies, candy, and cake got me through residency.

Interestingly, the Chicago group also found that sleeping four hours a night for six nights led to higher post-breakfast glucose levels than occurred after adequate sleep. Insulin secretion was compromised during sleep deprivation, cortisol levels rose and thyroid production declined. The results were almost suggestive of accelerated aging. Now that's scary. Fortunately, the men's glucose and insulin levels returned to normal after they had caught up on lost sleep.

Sleep Deprivation
and the Immune System

When was the last time you caught a cold or flu bug? Was it when you were well-rested after weeks on end of consistently wonderful sleep? Probably not. We're much more likely to succumb to a virus when we're run down, exhausted, and overextended. Getting adequate sleep is essential for maintaining a strong immune system. Conversely, immune function will be seriously compromised in the face of sleep debt.

Sleep deprivation makes most of us feel awful, but there is evidence that one rough night can take its toll on the immune system.[7] A study of 42 men at the University of California at San Diego, illustrates the point. After being allowed only a few hours sleep one night, the men's natural killer cell counts were significantly reduced. Similar research conducted in Australia a few years ago demonstrated as much as a 50% drop in lymphocyte counts after just one night of four hour's sleep. In both studies, cell counts returned to

38

normal after a good night of recovery sleep. These studies revealed a measurable problem in immune function after only one night of sleep deprivation. The bigger question remains – what really happens to people who are chronically sleep-deprived?

Over the last couple of years, we've had some challenges with a shortage of flu vaccine. There's been no shortage of reporting on it, but perhaps we should also pay attention to a lesser known problem. Evidence is pointing to a relationship between sleep and our response to vaccination. It appears that patients who are sleep-deprived mount a less effective immune response to influenza vaccine.[8] Vaccination plays a very important role in reducing morbidity and mortality, especially in the very young, the elderly, and folks with chronic illnesses. Perhaps we should make an effort to maximize the effectiveness of vaccines by recommending that people get plenty of rest before getting their shots!

The practice of medicine has long relied upon well-designed studies to guide our

The best science usually begins with observation.

treatments and recommendations. But the best science usually begins with observation. And for thousands of years, it's been observed that sick people usually sleep a lot, or at least they want to. Have you ever had a really nasty cold, flu, or pneumonia and conked out for 10 or 12 hours? Most of us have. Which brings us to another practical question. Why on earth do we torment people sick enough to be in a hospital by waking them up for vital signs? Sick people need their sleep more than they need us fussing at them. We can check their temperature and blood pressure when they wake up, not when we feel like waking them. Unless someone has just been admitted to the neuro-trauma unit with a head injury, we should let sleeping patients sleep. Do not wake patients for vital signs! Doctor's orders.

Neurologic Consequences of Sleep Deprivation

You might think that chronically sleep-deprived doctors would be very sympathetic to patients with sleep disorders, but such is not the case. In fact, the rigors of medical training seem to induce a cavalier, cynical attitude toward sleep loss. One particularly disconcerting study underscored the severity of the problem. Medical residents working long hours (averaging 32-hours at a stretch) had a 2.3 times greater likelihood of having a car accident, and a 5.9 times greater likelihood of having a "near miss" accident than residents who worked shorter hours.[9] Residents who routinely worked 24-hour or longer shifts made 35.9% more serious medical mistakes than when they worked more reasonable hours.[10] Those of us who are in the healthcare professions are supposed to be bright enough to learn from our mistakes. But large institutions are slow to change their policies and protocols, especially when money enters into the equation. Although scheduling has improved in recent years, interns and residents represent relatively cheap labor, so I doubt we'll be seeing 8- or 10-hour days any time soon.

Work-related errors are not the only consequence of sleep deprivation, however. Fatigue can compromise

Sleep deprivation can be downright deadly.

driving ability nearly as much as drunkness can. One study demonstrated that drivers who had gone 17 to 19 hours without sleep functioned like subjects with a blood alcohol level of 0.05%. For the sake of reference, a level of 0.08% is considered legally drunk in most states. Sleep-deprived drivers were far less quick and accurate in their responses than fully awake subjects.[11] According to the National Transportation Safety Board (NTSB), fatigue causes over 100,000 highway accidents each year. Sleep deprivation and resulting fatigue played a role in the disastrous Chernobyl accident, the Exxon Valdez oil spill, the space shuttle Challenger tragedy, and multiple serious ferry boat accidents in recent years.

Sleep deprivation can be downright deadly. But the very first symptoms of sleep deficit are decreased enthusiasm and creativity, along with increased irritability. Most of us know first hand that fatigue impairs our memory, attention span, and even comprehension. Not long ago, an interesting study revealed that sleepy individuals are more apt to make

Chapter 2 - Physiologic Consequences of Sleep Deprivation

poor decisions and take ill-advised risks than are their alert counterparts.[12] Stop for a moment and imagine what that would really do to your life.

Making poor decisions and taking inappropriate risks would eventually exact a heavy toll on your career, physical health and safety, financial well-being, family life, and friendships. There are consequences here that go far beyond feeling a little sleepy.

Sleep Deprivation
& the Musculoskeletal System:
Aches, Pains, & Falls

Virtually anyone who has even mild arthritis or fibromyalgia will agree that a restless night practically guarantees more pain the next day. Remember, many of the body's repair processes occur during deep, slow-wave sleep. Troublesome conditions like chronic fatigue syndrome and fibromyalgia (I can relate to both) are often associated with severely disrupted sleep architecture. We'll discuss the particulars in Chapter Three, but suffice it to say that aches and pains abound in the "wake" of sleep deprivation.

It stands to reason that orthopedic and post-op patients of any sort need good quality sleep to heal broken bones, torn ligaments, sprained muscles, and incisions. Serious athletes know that sleep deprivation can undermine months of rigorous training and literally ruin their competitive edge. It all goes back to basic physiology – most of our daily allotment of growth hormone is synthesized by the pituitary gland in Stage 4 deep sleep. Without an adequate supply of growth hormone, muscles turn to mush. The technical term is sarcopenia – strong, lean muscles turn into soft, weak flab. Sarcopenia is one of the hallmarks of aging. And the best way to prevent it is by combining regular exercise with good nutrition and sound sleep.

I must admit, however, that over the last three decades I've taken care of many more nursing home patients than competitive athletes. One of the biggest challenges in the former group is preventing falls. For decades, we preached about the dangers of sleeping pills leading to falls in the frail elderly. Obviously, oversedation and polypharmacy can be disastrous in older patients. But in 2005, a large and important study stirred considerable controversy on this subject. Of course it did. Anytime people think outside the box, controversy will ensue. The study involved 34,163 nursing home residents in Michigan. During a six-month period, researchers studied the risk of falls and hip fractures in patients with and without insomnia. Patients with insomnia were further categorized as to whether or not they used sleeping pills. The surprise came when statistical analysis revealed that insomnia, not sleeping pill use *per se*, was predictive of future falls.[13] That conclusion contradicts conventional medical wisdom that prescribing sleeping pills for the elderly increases their risk of falls. At least according to this study, the increased risk of falls may be attributable to the insomnia for which sleeping pills are often prescribed, rather than to the drugs themselves. In geriatrics circles, this is quite a revolutionary concept. Considering the increased options for newer non-benzodiazepine hypnotics today, it may well be time to liberalize our thinking about sleeping pill use. More to come on that subject in Chapter Nine.

The Dermatologic Consequences
of Sleep Deprivation

Medical journals aren't exactly bulging with studies on this one. But consider your own experience. Nearly everyone has had the occasional bad hair day. Take it a step further. Have you ever had a restless night when you tossed and turned and flopped like a fish? In the morning, you could have sworn by everything holy that you hadn't slept at all? Then you dragged yourself into the bathroom, looked in the mirror and thought, "Oh no! I'm having a bad face day." Perhaps you had deep circles and puffiness under your eyes; pale, sallow, ashy, or ruddy skin; a new blemish; or possibly a crease on the side of your face. In your teens and twenties, your skin recovers fairly quickly. But as the years pass, skin cell turnover slows down, new collagen production lags, estrogen levels falter, and connective tissues and subcutaneous fat decrease (too bad this doesn't happen in our hips). Toss in the fact that connective tissue, much like musculoskeletal tissue, repairs itself in slow-wave sleep, and the problem becomes quite clear. There's a reason people in various cultures have talked about the need for beauty sleep for centuries.

In recent years, dermatologists across the country have seen greater numbers of women in their 30s, 40s, and 50s with adult acne. There's no mystery here. When women are under stress they produce more catecholamines (adrenaline), more corstisol, and more testosterone. Our skin is not happy about this sequence of events. Oil glands can become overactive and clogged, with resulting inflammation. The entire process is exacerbated by sleep deprivation (which is exacerbated by overproduction of cortisol and adrenaline). Unfortunately, the most expensive face creams in the world can only do so much in the face of physiologic mayhem induced by exhaustion and stress.

Psychological Consequences of Sleep Deprivation

A few more studies have been conducted in this field over the last 15 or so years, but to a large extent, they've been thoroughly ignored. There is convincing evidence that insomnia increases the risk of current and future psychiatric disorders, especially anxiety and depression. For years, we've known that insomnia is often a symptom of depression. But the full extent of the problem is rarely appreciated. People who have major depression are more likely to be suicidal if they cannot sleep. [14] Thus, some physicians may be reluctant to treat insomnia because insomnia might be covering up the deeper problem of depression. Others have worried that sleeping pill use might make depression worse. That may have happened on occasion when older benzodiazepine hypnotics like Dalmane (flurazepam), Halcion (triazolam), or Restoril (temazepam) were used. But this simply doesn't seem to be a problem with the newer short-acting sleep medications.

In 2005, a ground-breaking trial looked at co-therapy for depression and insomnia in 545 patients who suffered from both conditions. Co-administration of fluoxetine (Prozac) and eszopiclone (Lunesta) was associated with larger and quicker improvements in both disorders than fluoxetine and placebo in a randomized controlled trial. The patients who received both drugs fell asleep more quickly, stayed asleep longer, and maintained sleep better than the control group. They also demonstrated greater improvement based on the Hamilton Depression Rating Scale. Even after two months of co-therapy, patients had no significant trouble with rebound insomnia or withdrawal effects.[15] These are important findings that should spark some thought about outmoded prescribing patterns.

It stands to reason that if treating insomnia enhances treatment of depression, that untreated insomnia could be really problematic. And now we have evidence of precisely that. Based on a study of 1,221 patients 65 years and older with major depressive disorders, chronic insomnia actually interferes with response to antidepressant therapy.[16] Bottom line: not only is chronic insomnia a precipitating factor for depression, it should now be viewed as a perpetuating factor as well.

Other studies have shown us that people who have trouble sleeping have greater difficulty coping with stress, completing projects, controlling their moods, and sustaining healthy personal and family relationships.[17] Absenteeism at work is greater in insomniacs than in control groups, and insomniacs are more dissatisfied with their jobs.[18] There is only one conclusion we can reach. It's nearly impossible to feel well, be well, or do well in the face of insomnia. But before we can address possible solutions, we need to define specific sleep disorders. And as we'll see in Chapter Three, the list is fairly lengthy.

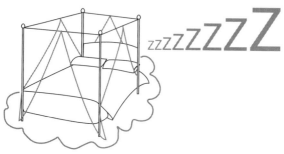

References

1. Dement W. *The Promise of Sleep*. New York, NY Delacourte Press, 1999.

2. Shamsuzzaman AS, Gersh BJ, Somers VK. Obstructive sleep apnea: implications for cardiac and vascular disease. *JAMA*, 2003; 290:1906-1914.

3. Gami AS, Pressman G, Caples SM, et al. Association of atrial fibrillation and obstructive sleep apnea. *Circulation*, 2004; 110: 364-367.

4. Meier-Ewert HK, Ridker PM, Rifai N, et al. Effect of sleep loss on C-reactive protein, an inflammatory marker of cardiovascular risk. *J Am Coll Cardiol*. 2004; 43: 678-683.

5. Yaggi HK, Concato J, Kernan WN, Lichtman JH, Brass LM, Mohsenin V. Obstructive sleep apnea as a risk factor for stroke and death. *N Eng J Med* 2005; 353: 2034-2041.

6. *Tufts University Health and Nutrition Letter* April 2005; 23(2). You Snooze, You Loose? Looking for the links between sleep, appetite and obesity.

7. Bryant PA, Trinder J. Curtis N. Sick and tired: Does sleep have a vital role in the immune system? *Nat Rev Immunol*. 2004; 4: 457-467.

8. Spiegel K, Sheridan JF, Van Cauter E. Effect of sleep deprivation on response to immunization [Letter]. *JAMA* 2002; 288: 1471-1472.

9. Barger LK, Cade BE, Ayas NT, et al. Extended work shifts and the risk of motor vehicle crashes among interns. *N Eng J Med*. 2005; 352: 125-34.

10. Landrigan CP, Rothschild JM, Cronin JW, et al. Effect of reducing intern's work hours on serious medical errors in intensive care units. *N Eng J Med*. 2004; 351: 838-48.

11. William AM, Feyer AM. Moderate sleep deprivation produces impairments in cognitive and motor performance equivalent to legally prescribed levels of alcohol intoxication. *Occup Environ Med*. 2000; 57: 649-55.

12. Roehrs T, Greenwald M, Roth T. Risk-taking behavior: effects of ethanol, caffeine and basal sleepiness. *Sleep*. 2004; 27: 887-893.

13. Avidan AY, et al. Insomnia and hypnotic use, recorded in the minimum data set, as predictors of falls and hip fractures in Michigan nursing homes. *J AM Geriatr Soc*. 2005; 53: 955-62.

14. Aragun MY, Kara H, Solmaz M. Subjective sleep quality and suicidality in patients with major depression. *J Psychiatr Res*. 1997; 31: 377-81.

15. Buysse DJ., et al. Comorbid Insomnia/Depression responds to cotherapy. Presented at the Annual meeting of the Associated Professional Sleep Societies. Reported in *Internal Medicine News*. Sep 1, 2005; p 24.

16. Pigeon W., et al. Insomnia curbs antidepressant response in aged. Presented at the annual meeting of Associated Professional Sleep Societies. Reported in *Internal Medicine News*. Sep 1, 2005: p 24.

17. The Gallup Organization. Sleep in America. 1995. reported in *Consultant*. Nov 2005.

18. Zammit GK, Weiner J, Damato N, et al. Quality of life in people with insomnia. *Sleep* 1999; 22 (suppl 2): 5379-5385.

Chapter 3

Sleep Disorders and Parasomnias

"He sleeps well who knows
not that he sleeps ill."

—Publilius Syrus
(1st Century B.C.)

Nearly one-third of our lives should be spent sleeping, and the quality of the other two-thirds will be profoundly affected by that sleep. Our moods, memory, judgment, work, and relationships depend on decent amounts and quality of sleep. And to be sure, every organ system in our body is dependent on sleep for optimal function. With that in mind, let's define some of the most troublesome disorders that interfere with much needed rest.

Insomnia: Defining the Terms

Insomnia is defined as difficulty with the initiation, maintenance, duration, or quality of sleep that results in the impairment of daytime functioning, despite adequate opportunity, and circumstances for sleep.[1] Transient insomnia lasts less than a week, short-term insomnia lasts one to four weeks, and chronic insomnia lasts over a month. Typically, chronic insomnia occurs more often in women, older individuals, and people with chronic illness. For years, insomnia was considered a relatively unimportant symptom. But specialists in the field of sleep medicine now consider insomnia to be a distinct disorder that's often associated with other medical conditions. Curiously, some people with insomnia are actually more alert during the daytime than are sound sleepers. This odd phenomenon is believed to be due to the state of hyperarousal that inhibits sleep during both daytime and nighttime. I know I can relate to this, and perhaps you can as well. Ever since medical school days, I've referred to this as the inability to turn off my brain. For years, I blamed it on my beeper, but I suspect many of us endure this dilemma simply because we're so over-stimulated in our culture.

In adults, insomnia is usually categorized as primary or secondary.[2]

The primary insomnias are as follows:

★ Idiopathic insomnia – idiopathic is a technical medical term that means, "We don't have a clue." Actually, this refers to insomnia which begins in infancy or childhood and has a persistent, unremitting course.

★ <u>Psychophysiologic insomnia</u> – often associated with a stressful or upsetting event, this condition of sleeplessness persists even after the problem is resolved. It reflects a maladaptive conditioned response, in which the patient learns to associate the bedroom with heightened arousal or worry, instead of sleep.

★ <u>Paradoxical insomnia</u> – is essentially sleep-state misperception. The patient's description of insomnia doesn't match objective polysomnographic (sleep study) findings.

The secondary insomnias (due to specific problems or conditions) are the following:

★ <u>Adjustment insomnia</u> – associated with current or active psychosocial stress.

★ <u>Inadequate sleep hygiene</u> – insomnia related to poor lifestyle habits that impair sleep.

★ <u>Insomnia because of a psychiatric disorder</u> – often a condition such as depression or anxiety.

★ <u>Insomnia because of a medical condition</u> – such as chronic pain, hot flashes, restless legs syndrome, nocturia, cough, or dyspnea.

★ <u>Insomnia because of a drug or substance</u> – may be precipitated by consuming or withdrawing from prescription medication, drugs of abuse, alcohol, or caffeine.

We'll discuss lifestyle, medication, and illness in greater detail later, but for now, let's define more sleep disorders.

Snoring

Depending on the circumstances, snoring can be amusing or infuriating if someone else is doing it, and downright embarrassing if the culprit is you. Medically speaking, snoring is partially obstructed breathing during sleep. It's a very common occurrence and fortunately, indicates sleep apnea only rarely. Severe or heavy snoring should be evaluated carefully for possible abnormalities in the neck, throat, pharynx, nose, and mouth. Snoring is far more common in obese people and is often aggravated by sleeping pills, tranquilizers, antihistamines, and, probably worst of all, alcohol.

Sleep Apnea Syndromes

Sleep apnea comes in three varieties: obstructive, central, and mixed. Each type involves cessation of breathing for 10 seconds or more, often 20 times an hour or more.[3] The end result is deoxygenation of blood, which takes a heavy toll on heart and brain function. People with any form of sleep apnea have higher mortality rates from myocardial infarction (MI) and stroke.[4] Other complications include problems with memory and cognition, hypertension, arrhythmias such as atrial flutter, bradycardia and ventricular tachycardia, congestive heart failure, and severe morning headaches. Extreme crankiness and irritability often accompany sleep apnea. Unfortunately, family members and physicians often fail to interpret these symptoms as warning signs of a potentially life-threatening condition. A more general term for sleep apnea is sleep-disordered breathing (SDB), which may occur in 25% of older adults.[5]

Obstructive sleep apnea is the most common form and ranges from mild to lethal. Men are affected more frequently than women, and typically they try to sleep in a supine position. Obesity contributes to blockage of the upper airway, cessation of breathing, choking, and then gasping, which awakens or arouses the patient. For the most part, patients are unaware of their frequent brief awakenings during the night, but they may be disturbed by excessive daytime sleepiness. Although obstructive sleep apnea is more common in middle-aged and older people, it does occur in children. Youngsters with enlarged tonsils and adenoids sometimes manifest this disorder, but they are mistakenly diagnosed as having attention-deficit/hyperactivity disorder (ADHD). The symptoms are very similar, but clearly sleep apnea won't be cured by Ritalin (methylphenidate)! The key here is awareness, a high index of suspicion, and a sleep study when in doubt.

Central sleep apnea or decreased respiratory drive can be seen in patients after a stroke, especially in the brain stem, or in association with other neurological illnesses such as Parkinson's, polio, or brain tumors in the posterior fossa. Perhaps you recall learning about Ondine's Curse in an ancient history or mythology course. Ondine's Curse, failure of brain stem breathing control, results in the inability to breathe adequately except when completely awake. The ancient gods surely could be vindictive.

Mixed sleep apnea includes aspects of both obstructive and central sleep apnea. It is generally treated as an obstructive condition.

Once the diagnosis is properly confirmed with a sleep study (polysomnography), several therapeutic interventions may be tried. In obese patients with obstructive sleep apnea, weight loss is crucial. It can reduce apneic spells, improve arterial gas levels, and improve daytime sleepiness. While the patient tries to lose weight, continuous positive airway pressure (CPAP) is used at night. The pressure used in CPAP must be carefully adjusted to eliminate apneic spells in various sleeping positions and all five stages of sleep. The device fits over the face and can be cumbersome to say the least, so compliance is often an issue. A newer device which is more streamlined and fits like a nasal oxygen cannula is available in some cases. When CPAP works, the patient and just about everyone else will know it within a night or two.

A variety of oral or dental appliances may be helpful as well. The mandibular advancement device pulls the lower jaw up and out, helping to open the upper airway more completely. Surgery, such as uvulopalatopharyngoplasty (often laser-assisted) is more of a last ditch effort, with no guarantee of success. But as is the case with virtually everything in medicine, you can't treat what you haven't diagnosed. And you can't diagnose a problem if you haven't even thought about it. When it comes to sleep apnea, nothing could be more vital.

Women tend to experience RLS more often than men.

Restless Legs Syndrome
& Periodic Limb Movement Disorder

Restless legs syndrome (RLS) is a neurologic movement disorder first described in the 1940's. Patients often struggle to describe their symptoms, but the fundamental problem is motor restlessness and unpleasant sensations in the legs that occur at rest. An estimated 12 million people suffer from this frustrating condition which clearly worsens with age. What doesn't?

Women tend to experience RLS more often than men, and symptoms can be exacerbated by stress and fatigue. Sensations can range from burning to itching to cramping to crawling. One lady told me it felt as if she had "club soda in her veins." The intensity of the sensations can vary from annoying to unbearable. In any event, the patient feels compelled to move her legs or walk around, but upon returning to bed, the distressing sensation returns.[6] Patients can virtually wear themselves out walking around the house at night. The next day, as you might expect, they're exhausted.

RLS is usually divided into two categories: primary and secondary. Most primary cases are probably familial and seem to have an autosomal dominant pattern of inheritance (inherited from mom or dad). Secondary RLS can be due to a number of other medical conditions [7]:

★ Iron deficiency (serum ferritin < 50 mg/ml).

★ Uremia.

★ B_{12} deficiency.

★ Peripheral neuropathy.

★ Pregnancy – especially last trimester.

★ Amyloidosis.

★ Diabetes.

★ Lumbosacral disc disease.

★ Parkinson's disease.

★ Lyme disease.

★ Rheumatoid arthritis.

★ Sjogren's syndrome.

★ Monoclonal gammopathy.

★ Medication: tricyclic antidepressants, selective serotonin reuptake inhibitors (SSRI's), lithium, dopamine antagonists.

Clearly, the best way to sort out the problem is to obtain a thorough history.

Approximately 80% of people with RLS experience periodic limb movement disorder (PLMD) as well.[8] PLMD involves jerking or twitching movements every 10 to 60 seconds, often just as the person is falling asleep.

A variety of medications can be tried for these frustrating disorders. Over the years, mild opioids and low-dose benzodiazepines have been used. A long-acting benzodiazepine, clonazepam (Klonopin) may help some patients. Anticonvulsant drugs such as carbamazepine (Tegretol) or gabapentin (Neurontin) have been used as well. More often, dopamine agonists used in Parkinson's disease have gained acceptance.[9] General examples include carbidopa-levodopa (Sinemet), pramipexole (Mirapex), and ropinirole

(Requip). Ropinirole and pramipexole have received specific Food and Drug Administration (FDA) approval for treatment of RLS. Side effects may include daytime drowsiness, fatigue, headache, and hypotension. These types of medications should not be stopped abruptly.

Non-drug measures which may offer a bit of relief include exercise in the daytime, massage, warm baths, or applied heat. Caffeine, alcohol, and smoking can make matters worse.

REM Behavior Disorder, Nightmares, & Night Terrors

Rapid eye movement (REM) behavior disorder is a fairly rare and bizarre sleep disorder that typically affects older men. It involves complex actions during sleep (i.e., talking, walking, and eating) that are accompanied by vivid and sometimes violent dreams. As you may recall, skeletal

Sleepwalking can occur in a calm or agitated manner with various degrees and complexity.

muscles are supposed to be paralyzed during REM sleep, so we don't act out our dreams. But for some unclear reason, that protective mechanism doesn't work in these patients. They may actually injure themselves or their partners during an unpleasant or disturbing dream. This, as you might expect, can be extremely upsetting and frightening for the spouse or partner.

Treatment usually involves clonazepam (Klonopin) 0.5 milligrams (mg) at bedtime. This long-acting benzodiazepine has been shown to inhibit abnormal body movements without specifically interfering with muscle tone.[10] Unfortunately, such a long-acting drug can cause falls in the elderly. If clonazepam cannot be used, low-dose desipramine can be tried. Regardless of the medication selected, the patient should be cautioned to place the mattress low or on the floor and remove any dangerous objects from the bedroom. In many cases, the only safe solution for the patient's partner is to sleep in a different room.

Night terrors are far more common in children than in adults and may be associated with sleepwalking. These distressing episodes often involve great fear, screaming, and flailing. Generally, night terrors occur during Stage 3 or 4 sleep. Adults can experience such episodes, and in many cases, they also have underlying psychological stresses or possibly alcoholism. Counseling and low dose benzodiazepines may be helpful.

Nightmares or frightening dreams also occur more often in children than in adults, but probably occur more often in women than in men. Nightmares are experienced during REM sleep and are commonly aggravated or precipitated by fever, exhaustion, alcohol, or various medications. Efforts to understand and address underlying psychological stresses are sometimes helpful. And avoiding violent television or scary movies just makes sense.

Sleepwalking

One of the most curious and sometimes frightening of the parasomnias is somnambulism, or sleepwalking. This disorder can occur in a calm or agitated manner with various degrees and complexity. The range of behavior includes walking aimlessly around the house, moving objects including furniture, eating inappropriately, wandering outdoors, and on the rare occasions, even driving a car! Usually patients have wide-open eyes with a dazed or glassy look. Episodes of sleepwalking may occur 15 to 120 minutes after onset of sleep in children, but they occur throughout the night in adults. At times, behavior may become very aggressive or frenetic, and the individual may become a danger to herself or others. Any of the parasomnias can be exacerbated by menstruation or pregnancy which suggests that hormonal fluctuations may play a role.

Enuresis

Nocturnal enuresis or bedwetting is sometimes associated with a variety of sleep disorders. It is more common in boys than in girls and seems to be familial. It can be a problem in about 30% of children at age four, about 10% at age six, and 3% at age 12. Enuresis usually reflects a delay in maturation of bladder control that resolves with time. Fortunately, only a small percentage of cases (1% to 2%) have a medical cause.

The most common etiology is a urinary tract infection. Other rare causes include diabetes mellitus or insipidus, sacral nerve pathology, congenital anomalies, or a pelvic mass. Depending upon findings from the history, physical and urine studies, further work-up may include a renal ultrasound, cystourethrogram, or other diagnostic evaluation. Enuresis can be caused by significant personal or family stress for which case psychotherapy or counseling may be required.

Young children with enuresis (up to age six) have high spontaneous cure rates, so treatment is not necessary. Spontaneous cure rates decline considerably after age six, however, so treatment becomes more urgent because of embarrassment. Motivational counseling with positive reinforcement for dry nights, having the child avoid drinking fluids two to three hours before bedtime, and reassurance to avoid blame and guilt are helpful. Enuresis alarms are triggered by a few drops of urine and gradually condition the child to inhibit urination. Short-term use of desmopressin nasal spray (synthetic antidiuretic hormone) may be useful in children over age six.

Jet Lag & Shift Work Sleep Disorder

Jet lag and shift work are both notorious for disrupting normal sleep. Also known as circadian rhythm sleep disorders, jet lag and shift work reflect a disconnect between internal sleep-wake cycles and the environment. Most patients will have insomnia and excessive daytime sleepiness that eventually resolve once their internal clocks have adapted.

Jet lag can develop after travel across two or more time zones. Traveling east and advancing the sleep cycle causes more troublesome symptoms than traveling west and delaying sleep. Fatigue, headache, gastrointestinal (GI) disturbances, and malaise can be significant, to say the least. Sleep disruption in jet lag is exacerbated by a desynchronization of cortisol production, thyroid levels, melatonin synthesis, and body temperature curves.[11] Typically, recovering from jet lag requires approximately one day for each time zone crossed.

Before travel, it's helpful to shift one's sleep-wake cycle gradually to approximate that of the destination. Upon

Try to be around bright light at work.

arrival, the most useful strategy is to maximize exposure to bright morning light. Minimizing caffeine and alcohol and walking or exercising outdoors can help as well. Appropriately timed use of melatonin, or prescription sleep medications for rest (or modafinil to stay awake), may be useful for limited periods of time.

Jet lag can certainly be unpleasant, but sleep loss due to shift work is usually worse. Over 20% of us work evening or night shifts. People in health care, communications, transit, security, police work, firefighting, and rescue work either rotate shifts or work routinely at night. If you have to be on call, you probably work day and night. Oh joy! It's estimated that 60% to 70% of shift workers struggle with sleep disturbances. The severity of symptoms is related to the frequency of shift changes and the frequency of counter-clockwise changes (advancing the sleep time).[12] Much of the problem is due to daytime noise and light and what can seem like endless interruptions from ringing phones, doorbells, faxes, barking dogs, and noisy neighbors.

Unfortunately, shift workers who are sleep-deprived tend to fall asleep more often on the job and can make some catastrophic mistakes. Doctors make more errors in judgment or prescribing medications incorrectly. As described in Chapter One, devastating accidents have occurred in the wake of sleep deprivation related to shift work.

There are a few strategies that shift workers may find helpful. When possible, stay on the same shift week in and week out. If rotating shifts are mandatory, people should rotate from day to evening to night and stay on the same shift for two weeks at a time. Before leaving work, put on the darkest wraparound sunglasses that you can find. Once bright daylight hits the retina, a message is sent to the pineal gland to reduce melatonin production. Wrong message! Try to be around bright light at work (at least in non-patient care areas). Once you arrive home, take a bath or shower, have a bite to eat and go to bed. Dark curtains or black-out shades and use of an eye mask may be helpful. Had it not been for earplugs over the years, I would now be insane. Some people like white noise machines or nature sounds to mask ambient noise. Resist the temptation to revert to old sleeping schedules on days off. The folks who are best equipped physiologically to work nights are natural-born night owls. If you know in your heart you're a *bona fide* morning person, working nights will make you feel like a salmon swimming upstream. May I recommend that you stop working nights immediately! Life is too short to make yourself ill doing something for which you're not suited.

Delayed & Advanced Sleep Phase Syndromes

If you've ever had the feeling you weren't going to bed at the right time, you may have had one of these frustrating syndromes. Delayed sleep phase syndrome occurs mostly in children, teenagers, and 20-somethings. Typically, young people with the problem stay up until 2:00 am or 3:00 am

Most patients with alpha wave intrusion disorder need at least a brief course of sleep medication.

watching television, talking on the phone or sitting in front of a computer. But then they're unable to get up in time for school. When they do try to go to bed earlier, they simply can't fall asleep. The consequences, in terms of academic performance and even mood and social interaction, can be significant.

Treatment of delayed sleep phase syndrome is fairly low tech. Exposure to very bright light very early in the morning is key. Bedtime should be advanced 15 to 20 minutes every few nights (in a gradual fashion) until falling asleep at an appropriate hour becomes feasible. It's important to note that delayed sleep phase syndrome can also be problematic for adults with chronic illness. A classic example would be patients with chronic fatigue syndrome or fibromyalgia. More on those conditions later.

People with advanced sleep phase syndrome have the opposite problem. They can scarcely keep their eyes open by 7:00 pm or 8:00 pm, but by 3:00 am, they're wide-awake and unable to go back to sleep. The pattern is quite common in older individuals. Treatment involves exposure to bright light as late as possible in the afternoon and evening and gradually delaying bedtime by 15 to 20 minutes every few nights. And no falling asleep with the television on!

Alpha Wave Intrusion Disorder

This little known, but frustrating, sleep disorder is very common in patients with chronic fatigue syndrome and fibromyalgia. Typically, these individuals have difficulty falling asleep when they need to (delayed sleep phase syndrome). But when they finally do drift off, their sleep architecture is badly disturbed. They may toss and turn all night long, and in the morning be quite certain they have not slept at all. Apparently, as soon as they start to flirt with Stage 3 or 4 sleep, their brain launches a burst of alpha waves which "intrude" into slow-wave sleep, and they revert to light Stage 1 or 2 sleep. Not very refreshing. This disorder obviously can only be diagnosed in a sleep lab, so the vast majority of people who suffer from it never fully understand precisely what the problem is.

Although good sleep hygiene measures may help a bit, most patients need at least a brief course of sleep medication.

Over the past 12 to 15 years zolpidem (Ambien) or zaleplon (Sonata) have proven to be useful, since they allow patients to enter Stage 4 sleep. We'll discuss the details more in Chapter Seven.

Alpha wave intrusion disorder can only be diagnosed in a sleep lab.

Fatal Familial Insomnia

This rather frightening condition is very a rare, progressive, degenerative disorder of the thalamus. Fatal familial insomnia is a multi-symptom illness associated with autonomic instability and marked fluctuations in consciousness. These patients are extremely ill and unable to function in a home setting. Most cases involve an autosomal dominant mutation, with an average onset around age 40. Early symptoms include trouble falling asleep, intermittent myoclonus, or muscle spasms. Eventually, autonomic symptoms develop including severe hypertension, sweating, tachycardia, and hyperthermia. Dementia becomes prominent over a period of months, and death often occurs within 12 to 15 months. Genetic testing is used to confirm the diagnosis.

Narcolepsy

Narcolepsy is a disorder of sleep-wake regulation which often begins around puberty. The term dates back to the year 1880, but only recently has a probable etiology been identified. Virtually everyone with narcolepsy has extremely low or undetectable levels of hypocretin, a hormone involved in control of alertness.[13] The illness seems to be related to auto-immune destruction of hypocretin-containing neurons in the lateral hypothalamus. Genetic and environmental factors probably play a role.

A key feature of narcolepsy is dysregulation of the timing and control of REM sleep. Consequently, REM sleep intrudes on other activities at peculiar or even dangerous times. A person may suddenly fall into REM sleep while sitting in a seminar, talking in an interview, or driving a car. Willpower and good sleep habits have no impact on the problem.

Narcolepsy affects both genders and all races equally.

Typically, the individual experiences puzzling symptoms for five or 10 years before the diagnosis is made. Diagnosis requires evaluation in a sleep lab.

Symptoms follow a chronic and relentless course and may include any of the following:

★ Excessive daytime sleepiness.

★ Sleep attacks during normal daytime activities.

★ Disturbed nighttime sleep (unwanted awakenings).

★ Automatic behaviors – performing routine tasks without being aware of what one is doing (unloading the dishwasher but placing dishes in the fridge).

★ Cataplexy – complete loss of muscle tone or paralysis while alert; often precipitated by strong emotions like surprise, anger, or laughter.

★ Sleep paralysis – when REM sleep begins during the transition between wakefulness and actual sleep a terrifying feeling of paralysis can occur.

★ Hypnagogic hallucinations – onset of REM dreams just before falling asleep or waking up; patients may not be able to distinguish these images from reality.

A thorough work-up is very important since hypersomnia can be due to many conditions, including brain tumors, multiple sclerosis, encephalitis, hypothyroidism, glucose abnormalities, anemia, uremia, seizure disorders, hepatic failure, or hypercalcemia.

Unfortunately, there is no cure for narcolepsy. Some patients respond, at least partially, to 15 to 20 minute naps every few hours. Such an approach, however, is impractical for many people. Stimulant medications like methylphenidate (Ritalin) pemoline (Cylert), and dextroamphetamine (Dexedrine) may help combat drowsiness and sleep attacks. Antidepressants that suppress REM sleep such as fluoxetine (Prozac), sertraline (Zoloft), paroxetine (Paxil), or venlafaxine (Effexor) sometimes help prevent cataplexy. In 1999, the Food and Drug Administration (FDA) approved modafinil (Provigil), a long-acting drug that promotes wakefulness. It is not a stimulant drug. Modafinil is given in a 100 to 200 mg dose in the morning. Doses are gradually increased as needed. Euphoria and weight loss are not side effects of modafinil, so there is much less potential for abuse. The latest drug for cataplexy is sodium oxybate (Xyrem), also know as GHB (gamma hydroxybutyrate).[14] GHB has a dark side as the "date rape" drug. In the setting of narcolepsy with cataplexy, it can be helpful. Obviously, Xyrem is very tightly controlled as it should be.

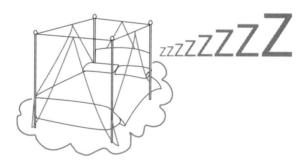

References

1. Costa e Silva J A, Chase M, Sartorius N, et al. Special report from a symposium held by the World Health Organization and the World Federation of Sleep Research Societies: an overview of insomnias and related disorders – recognition, epidemiology, and national management. *Sleep*. 1996; 19(5): 412-416.

2. *The International Classification of Sleep Disorders: Diagnostic and Coding Manual*, ICDS-2. 2nd ed. Westchester, III: American Academy of Sleep Medicine, 2005.

3. American Academy of Sleep Medicine Task Force. Sleep-related breathing disorders in adults: Recommendations for syndrome definition and measurement techniques in clinical research. *Sleep*. 1999; 22: 667-689.

4. Yaggi HK, Concato J, Kernan WN, et al. Obstructive sleep apnea as a risk factor for stroke and death. *N Engl J Med*. 2005: 353: (19). 2034-2041.

5. Ancoli-Israel S. Kripke DF, Klauber MR, et al. Sleep-disordered breathing in community-dwelling elderly. *Sleep*. 1991; 14(6): 486-495.

6. Allen R P, Picchiette D, Hening W A, et al. Restless legs syndrome: Diagnostic criteria, special considerations and epidemiology. *Sleep Med*. 2003; 4:101-119.

7. Gianikos DG, Harwood R. Restless legs syndrome. *Patient Care*. 2005. June; 13-14.

8. Ancoli-Israel S, Kripke D F, Klauber MR, et al. Periodic limb movements in sleep in community-dwelling elderly. *Sleep*. 1991;14:496-500.

9. Earley CJ. Clinical practice: Restless leg syndrome. *N Engl J Med*. 2003; 348: 2103-2109.

10. Cohen-Zion M, Ancoli-Israel S. Sleep disorders. In: Hazzard UR, Blass JP, Halter JB, et al. *Principles of Geriatric Medicine and Gerontology*, 5th ed. New York, NY: McGraw-Hill, Inc; 2003: 1531-1541.

11. Czeisber CA, Klerman EB. Circadian and sleep-dependent regulation of hormone release in humans. *Rec Prog Hormone Res.* 1999; 54: 97-132.

12. American Sleep Disorders Associations. The International Classification of Sleep Disorders: Diagnostic and Coding Manual 2nd ed. Westchester, SU. The American Academy of Sleep Medicine. 2005.

13. Nishino S, Ripley B, Overeem S, et al. Hypocretin (orexin) deficiency in human narcolepsy. *Lancet.* 2000; 355:39-40.

14. Guilleminault C, Fromberz S. Narcolepsy: diagnosis and management. In Krugger MR, Roth T, Dement W, eds. *Principles and Practice of Sleep Medicine.* 4th ed. Philadelphia, PA: Elsevier/Saunders; 2005:780-790.

Chapter 4

Sleep Studies and the Diagnostic Evaluation

"There ain't no way to find out why a snorer can't hear himself snore."

—Mark Twain (1894)
Tom Sawyer Abroad

Pop quiz! If 66% of Americans are having problems sleeping, but fewer than 3% are seeing a physician for help, what on earth are the other 63% doing?

A.   Having a few too many nightcaps

B.   Marinading in over-the-counter antihistamines

C.   Watching really bad late night infomercials

D.   All of the above

The correct answer is D, which actually means most people are suffering in silence, enduring more illness and accidents, being less productive, and experiencing far less enjoyment in life. And since most American physicians have negligible training in sleep disorders and rarely even ask patients about sleep, those of us with sleep problems simply must speak up. After all, the most brilliant doctors in the world can't read your mind. Let's discuss when it's time to get help.

When Is a Medical Evaluation Indicated?

According to the American Academy of Sleep Medicine, one should obtain medical help if sleep deprivation has compromised daytime functioning for more than one month. Over the years, I've relied on two practical questions for patients:

1.   Are you sleeping well at night?
2.   Do you have the energy to do what you want or need to do in the daytime?

This may not sound very scientific, but there's a difference between not having the energy to go to work and not having the energy to go shopping. When someone doesn't feel well enough to do the things she'd love to do, then something is wrong. Few things in medicine are more simple than that.

Clues From the History & Physical Exam

A thorough insomnia or sleep-disorder history can take between 30 and 60 minutes.[2] No one can tackle this problem in a seven-minute office visit, so it would be useful to review these questions before a trip to the doctor:

1. When did the symptoms begin? Are they getting worse?

2. Is there a pattern of insomnia – is it every night or is it sporadic?

3. Do you have difficulty falling asleep, staying asleep, or waking up too early?

4. How long do you stay awake during episodes of sleep deprivation?

5. Is your insomnia related to menstrual cycles, hot flashes, or pregnancy?

6. What are the daytime consequences of your insomnia (i.e., irritability, memory lapses, trouble concentrating, fatigue, or sleepiness)?

7. Are you under any unusual stress now (i.e., job loss or change, marital or relationship problems, death in the family, personal or family illness, or financial crisis)?

8. Does your spouse, partner, or other persons close to you realize your sleep is disturbed?

Many medical conditions and illnesses can take a heavy toll on sleep. A thorough "review of systems" should help pinpoint the problem, but if your doctor doesn't ask, you should volunteer pertinent information:

1. Do you experience indigestion or heartburn at night?

2. Are you bothered by nasal congestion or allergy symptoms at night?

3. Do you ever wake up during the night with coughing or shortness of breath or chest pain?

4. Are you bothered by uncomfortable, fidgety sensations in your legs or feet at night?

5. Do you feel restless, kick, or thrash around at night?

6. Do you ever wake up with a headache?

7. Is your sleep disrupted by frequent trips to the bathroom?

8. Do hot flashes frequently disturb your sleep?

The answers to these questions will help guide the physical exam, possible lab work, and other diagnostic studies.

But before launching into any costly tests, there are even more questions to be asked about habits and lifestyle:

1. How would you describe a typical night's sleep?

2. What is your usual evening routine?

3. What time do you generally go to bed and wake up?

4. How long does it take you to fall asleep?

5. How often do you wake up during the night? Do you usually get out of bed during those episodes?

6. Is your weekend sleep routine much different from your weekday regimen?

7. What is your bedroom like?

8. Do you work erratic shifts or travel frequently?

9. Do you often fall asleep in another room?

10. Can you sleep well on vacation or in a hotel room?

11. Do you consume much caffeine, alcohol, or nicotine?

12. What do you usually eat or drink before bedtime?

13. Do you ever take naps in the daytime?

14. What is your typical day like?

15. How do you relax after work? (Don't laugh so hard.)

16. Do you spend time outside most days?

17. Is exercise a part of your daily routine? When do you generally work out or walk?

18. Are you exposed to bright light in the evening?

19. How would you describe your home environment?

20. Do you often feel drowsy during the day?

21. Do you ever fall asleep at work or nod off while driving?

Upon completing a thorough sleep history (which can easily take an hour), a focused physical examination should be done. The cardiovascular examination is vital to help rule out serious causes of insomnia such as congestive heart failure, valvular disease, angina, peripheral arterial disease (PAD), or arrhythmias. The pulmonary examination is directed at possible culprits like allergies, obstructive sleep apnea, asthma, and chronic obstructive pulmonary disease (COPD). Based on findings from the history and physical examination, appropriate tests can be ordered. Often these tests would include a chemistry panel with attention to the glucose level, blood urea nitrogen (BUN), and creatinine to screen for renal disease. A complete blood count (CBC) is useful to screen for anemia or possible infection. In older patients or those with chronic illness, a chest x-ray (CXR), and electrocardiogram (EKG) may be indicated. Additional tests such as thyroid levels (TSH), sedimentation rate (sed rate), anti-nuclear antibodies (ANA), and rheumatoid arthritis (RA) may be helpful, based on the history and physical examination. Fortunately, the vast majority of patients with a sleep problem can be helped without resorting to more costly, invasive testing.

Keeping a Sleep Journal

An excellent way to streamline the diagnostic work-up and get the most out of an office visit is to keep a sleep journal or diary. Ideally, your sleep-wake patterns over a two-week period should be recorded. This is a very practical way to develop insight into the true nature of the sleep problem. Best results are obtained when the following questions are answered first thing in the morning (or upon wakening).

A Sample Sleep Journal

Name: _____

Date: _____

1. What time did you go to bed last night?
    time: _____

2. How long did it take you to fall asleep?
    _____ hours _____ minutes

3. How many times did you wake
   up during the night?
    amount of awakenings: _____

4. How long did it take you to fall asleep
   again each time you woke up?
    1st awakening _____ hours _____ minutes
    2nd awakening _____ hours _____ minutes
    3rd awakening _____ hours _____ minutes
    4th awakening _____ hours _____ minutes
    5th awakening _____ hours _____ minutes

5. What time did you wake up this morning?
    time: _____

6. What time did you get out of bed this morning?
    time: _____

7. How much difficulty did you experience
   falling asleep last night?
    1 – Great difficulty
    2 – Moderate difficulty
    3 – Some difficulty

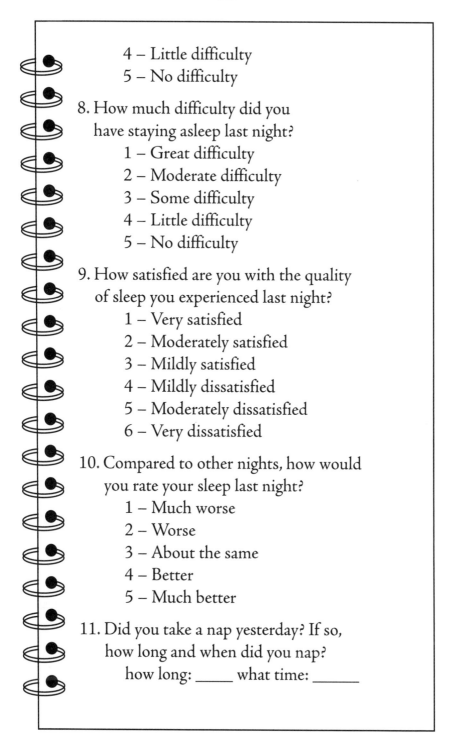

4 – Little difficulty
5 – No difficulty

8. How much difficulty did you
   have staying asleep last night?
   1 – Great difficulty
   2 – Moderate difficulty
   3 – Some difficulty
   4 – Little difficulty
   5 – No difficulty

9. How satisfied are you with the quality
   of sleep you experienced last night?
   1 – Very satisfied
   2 – Moderately satisfied
   3 – Mildly satisfied
   4 – Mildly dissatisfied
   5 – Moderately dissatisfied
   6 – Very dissatisfied

10. Compared to other nights, how would
    you rate your sleep last night?
    1 – Much worse
    2 – Worse
    3 – About the same
    4 – Better
    5 – Much better

11. Did you take a nap yesterday? If so,
    how long and when did you nap?
    how long: _____ what time: _____

12. Did you take anything to
    help you sleep last night?

    Prescription medication?

    _____

    _____

    Over-the-counter medication?

    _____

    _____

    Herbal supplement?

    _____

    _____

    Alcohol?

    _____

    _____

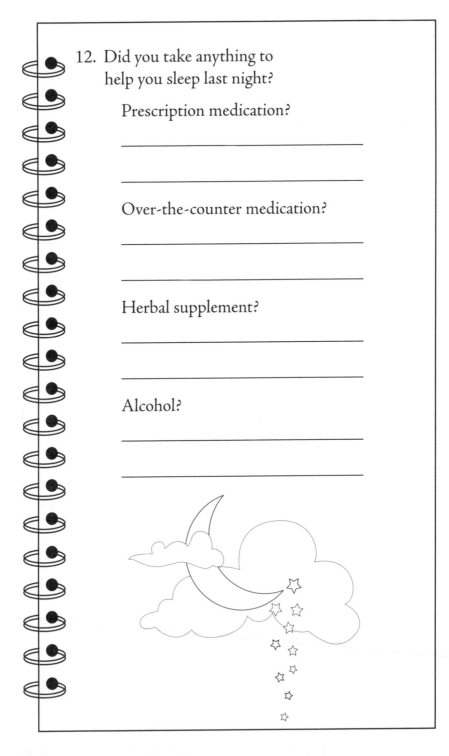

The Epworth Sleepiness Scale

Another useful addition to the diagnostic evaluation is the Epworth Sleepiness Scale.[3] This Epworth Scale is one of the few symptom-rating scales that has been validated against a true physiologic standard—the Multiple Sleep Latency Test.[4] A score of greater than 16 is indicative of excessive daytime sleepiness and the need for a thorough examination beyond a basic history and physical.

How likely are you to doze off or fall asleep in the following situations, as opposed to feeling just tired? This refers to your usual way of life in recent times. Even if you have not done some of these things recently, try to determine how they would have affected you. Use this scale to choose the most appropriate number for each situation.

Fortunately, most people with a sleep problem can be helped without an overnight stay in a sleep lab.

Table 1. The Epworth Sleepiness Scale

0 = no chance of dozing

1 = slight chance of dozing

2 = moderate chance of dozing

3 = high chance of dozing

Situation	Chance of Dozing
Sitting and reading	
Watching TV	
Sitting inactively in a public place (such as in a theater or in a meeting)	
Lying down to rest in the afternoon when circumstances permit	
Sitting and talking to someone	
In a car, while stopped for a few minutes in traffic	

Reprinted with permission from *Sleep* by Johns, MW. Copyright 1991 by Am Acad of Sleep Medicine.

What Happens in a Sleep Lab?

Fortunately, most people with a sleep problem can be helped without an overnight stay in a sleep lab. Primary insomnia and circadian rhythm disturbances can usually be diagnosed with a good history. When a more serious sleep disorder is suspected (i.e., narcolepsy, sleep apnea, or periodic limb movement disorder), formal sleep studies are often warranted.

The gold standard for assessing sleep is polysomnography. Typically, this includes monitoring electroencephalography (EEG), electromyogram (EMG) of chin and leg muscles, and electrooculogram (EOG). EOG records eye movements. These measurements are usually supplemented with pulse oximetry, electrocardiogram (EKG), and measurements of nasal and oral airflow and respiratory effort.

An overnight stay in a sleep lab is not exactly a spa experience. More often than not, a physician referral is required, and appropriate medical records are requested beforehand. A sleep journal or questionnaire is sent out to the patient for completion before testing. During the visit the patient can wear her own nightclothes and bring her own pillow from home. Audio and visual taping will occur

An overnight stay in a sleep lab is not exactly a spa experience.

during the night to record snoring, talking during sleep, and any evidence of movement disorders such as restless legs or periodic limb movement disorder. All of this is a good excuse to buy new jammies. After the technician sets up the monitoring devices, the patient is allowed to relax alone until bedtime. Readings are monitored throughout the night in a control room which is usually next door.

All of the data are recorded on a single printout (the polysomnogram) and reviewed by both the technician and the physician. When there is clear evidence of a respiratory problem early in the sleep study, treatment such as CPAP (continuous positive airway pressure) will be tried to see if a therapeutic response occurs. In more complex cases, a second night of sleep studies may be required. In fact, daytime sleep studies may be indicated, especially if narcolepsy is suspected or if daytime sleepiness has been a problem. The multiple sleep latency test measures the time necessary to fall asleep while resting in a quiet room, and which stages of sleep occur during a short nap. The protocol is generally conducted four or five times throughout the day in two-hour intervals. As a rule of thumb, a patient who falls asleep each time in five minutes or less has extreme daytime sleepiness.

In recent years, sleep-monitoring equipment has been developed for home use. Opinions vary as to the reliability of the information gathered since the home devices can miss mild sleep apnea.[5] Nevertheless, home-based sleep testing can be very helpful in frail, elderly patients. It can help bedridden or handicapped individuals. It can be done even after formal sleep studies to evaluate the effectiveness of therapy.

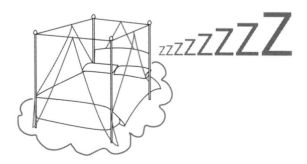

Chapter 4 - Sleep Studies and the Diagnostic Evaluation

References

1. Haponik EF, Frye AW, Richards B, et al. Sleep history is neglected diagnostic information. Challenges for primary care physicians. *J Gen Intern Med*. 1996;11(12):759-761.

2. O'Keefe ST, Gavin K, Lavan JN. Iron status and restless legs syndrome in the elderly. *Age Ageing* 1994;23(3):200-203.

3. Johns MW. A new method for measuring daytime sleepiness: the Epworth sleepiness scale. *Sleep*. 1991;14(6):540-545.

4. Chervin RD, Aldrich MS, Pickett R, et al. Comparison of the results of the Epworth Sleepiness Scale and the Multiple Sleep Latency Test. *J Psychosom Res* 1997;42(4):145-155.

5. Edinger JD, Glenn DM, Bastian LA, et al. Sleep in the laboratory and sleep at home II: comparisons of middle-aged insomnia sufferers and normal sleepers. *Sleep*. 2001;24(7):761-770.

Chapter 5

Medical Conditions That Disrupt Sleep

"Sleep to the sick is half health."

—German Proverb

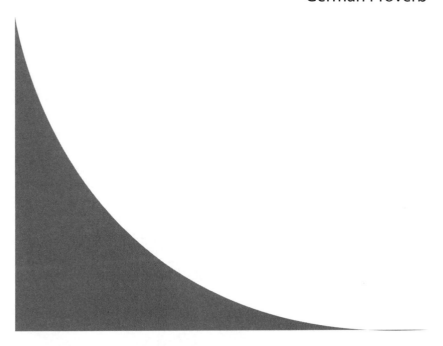

Anyone who has ever had a nasty cold or flu-bug knows how maddening it is to be too sick to sleep. You're so exhausted you feel as if you need to sleep for a week, but aches and pains and congestion and coughing leave you marinading in wakeful misery. Five or six frustrating nights like this are more than enough. But a long list of chronic illnesses — cardiovascular, respiratory, metabolic, neurologic, rheumatologic, or gastrointestinal — can contribute to long, restless nights, difficult, exhausting days, and continual deterioration in health. While medical problems can disrupt sleep at any age, those of us in mid-life and beyond tend to have multiple medical challenges. There is no doubt that sleep quality declines as more medical conditions develop. In 2003, the famous "Sleep in America" survey discovered that 36% of people over 65 years old with no health problems had sleep disturbances, 52% of those with one to three comorbid illnesses had a sleep disturbance, and 69% of folks with four or more concurrent medical problems had trouble sleeping. Overall, the more illnesses people had, the worse they felt their sleep was.[1]

Sleep problems related to an underlying medical diagnosis are often described as secondary insomnia. In 2005, the State-of-the-Science Conference on Insomnia sponsored by the National Institutes of Health (NIH) recognized this important and widespread clinical challenge and recommended using the term "comorbid insomnia."[2]

Regardless of the clinical term currently used, the relationship between chronic medical illness and sleep deprivation is complex. A long list of symptoms such as pain, cough, shortness of breath, paresthesias, and urinary frequency, just to name a few, exacerbate changes in the brain that seem to create a two-way vicious circle. Illness makes insomnia worse and insomnia aggravates illness. The interplay between the two is undoubtedly more significant than we usually acknowledge in everyday practice. And yet, it may determine whether or not recovery occurs.

At the most basic level, being sick produces symptoms of emotional distress and physical discomfort that activate neural pathways that control sleep and wakefulness. The combination of being stressed out, over-stimulated, and uncomfortable, together with certain personality traits and reduced coping skills, aggravate insomnia even more. Unfortunately, once sleep problems are labeled as a consequence of physical or emotional illness, they tend to be overlooked and undertreated.[3,4] This is when the vicious circle intensifies. Sustained sleep impairment often increases morbidity and even mortality in patients with chronic illness. For the sake of both enhanced quality of life and more effective treatment, addressing the challenge of "comorbid insomnia" becomes vitally important.

Respiratory Disorders That Disrupt Sleep

Respiratory illness and sleep disorders are commonly found in the same patient. Oxygen levels in the blood may be slightly diminished during sleep, especially in the setting of asthma and chronic obstructive pulmonary disease (COPD). This is where the vicious cycle kicks in. Low arterial oxygen saturation levels can compromise sleep quality and increase central nervous system (CNS) irritability. In normal-person English, the worse your respiratory illness is, the less you sleep. The less you sleep, the worse your respiratory illness becomes.

The classic symptoms of obstructive sleep apnea are: snoring; daytime sleepiness; interrupted or fragmented sleep; and poor sleep quality. About 25% of people with COPD experience excessive daytime sleepiness. During rapid eye movement (REM) sleep (dreaming), their blood oxygen levels dip to low levels, and they tend to wake up. Unfortunately, even treatment with oxygen at night fails to improve their sleep quality despite better blood levels of oxygen.[5] This is perplexing at first glance, but patients with COPD have many reasons for disrupted sleep, including cough, dyspnea, and copious respiratory secretions. A helpful strategy in these patients is using an inhaler with ipratropium bromide (Atrovent) to improve airflow and consequently enhance sleep quality and duration.[6]

> Illness makes insomnia worse and insomnia aggravates illness.

COPD is not the only respiratory problem capable of disturbing sleep, however. Anything from pneumonia to

Chapter 5 - Medical Conditions That Disrupt Sleep

bronchitis to a sinus infection, allergy, or a garden-variety cold can be the culprit. Temporarily suppressing cough and relieving nasal congestion, especially at night, can bring blessed relief and much needed sleep. Of course, these days it's more difficult to buy over-the-counter products containing the useful decongestant pseudoephedrine (phenylephrine used in its place is not nearly as effective). Tight controls went into effect in the spring of 2006 in an attempt to counter illegal crystal methamphetamine production. Chances are good, however, that if you're reading this book you are not running a crystal methamphetamine lab in your basement. Sometimes the regulatory types go overboard. Perhaps they don't remember the last time they had a really bad cold.

Cardiovascular Disorders that Disrupt Sleep

If you've ever spent time in a cardiac unit as a patient, a visitor, or staff, you know that sleep can be a precious and rare experience in the setting of heart disease. Hospital distractions and noise aside, the physiologic disruptions induced by ischemia, valvular heart disease, arrhythmias, cardiomyopathy, and congestive heart failure often result in sleep-deprived, restless, uncomfortable nights, and exhausting days. Once again, we see the vicious cycle concept rear its ugly head. Chronic trouble falling asleep correlates with an increased risk of dying from cardiovascular disease.[7] We've also known for some time that a circadian peak of ischemia or myocardial infarction (MI) occurs between 4:00 am and 8:00 am. If you've ever worked in an emergency room, you've observed this many times.

One of the most common cardiac conditions that classically disrupts sleep is congestive heart failure. In fact, even when taking a history from a patient, we focus heavily on the presence of two specific nighttime symptoms – (1) orthopnea, and (2) paroxysmal nocturnal dyspnea. Two specific disturbances contribute to the insomnia of congestive heart failure (CHF). First, spending a few hours supine causes blood to be redistributed from the extremities to the heart and lungs. Fluid backs up, causing congestion and sudden middle-of-the-night awakening and gasping for breath. Sometimes patients with CHF will wake up abruptly, sit up, stand up, or even hang halfway out a window trying to catch a good breath. This is classic paroxysmal nocturnal dyspnea (PND). It's always important in medicine to be careful about abbreviations. PND to a cardiologist means paroxysmal nocturnal dyspnea. PND to an otolaryngologist means post-nasal drip!

The second disturbance in CHF related to insomnia is a phenomenon known as Cheyne-Stokes respiration. This is an irregular pattern of breathing that fragments sleep and results in daytime fatigue and sleepiness. Cheyne-Stokes respiration correlates with a worsened prognosis and increased cardiac death.[8,9] Sometimes a patient with Cheyne-Stokes respiration will wake up abruptly with a disturbing sense of breathlessness.[10] Over the years, clinicians have also observed that many patients with hypertension (common in angina and CHF patients) often complain of insomnia. It's not entirely clear how much of this is due to medications such as diuretics, associated obesity, or other conditions. Lastly, we know that patients who have undergone coronary artery bypass surgery often have difficulty sleeping as long as two years after their procedure.[11] This is probably due to many factors, including post-operation pain, tender scar tissue, stress, medications, poor but deeply engrained sleep habits, and anxiety. Considering the prevalence of heart disease in general, we shouldn't be surprised that insomnia torments so many people in mid-life and beyond.

GI Disorders that Disrupt Sleep

The gastrointestinal (GI) tract includes everything from the mouth to the anus. Anything amiss in any structure along the way can cause more than enough misery to disrupt sleep. Whether the problem is as serious as Crohn's disease or ulcerative colitis or as mundane as gas pains, sleep can become a long-term casualty.

One of the most common GI disorders that disrupts sleep is gastroesophageal reflux disease, or GERD. This term has gone from conference room lingo to living room conversations courtesy of endless commercials over the past seven or eight years.

Symptoms of GERD occur when gastric acid flows backward and up into the esophagus, which is not anatomically equipped to handle the low pH. Reflux can certainly occur during the daytime (often bending over or stooping down to pick up something or cleaning a floor or bathroom – cleaning can be bad for you!). But in some patients, reflux occurs only during sleep. Unfortunately, when someone has a dysfunctional or incompetent lower esophageal sphincter, the arousal process becomes essential in allowing adequate clearance of acid from the esophagus. Great! Just as you finally drift asleep you wake up with a jolt, coughing, gagging, sputtering, and otherwise being generally restless and miserable. Sometimes people can have profound reflux without overt feelings of heartburn.[12] This is really important to understand. Chronic nighttime restlessness in the absence of other obvious problems should always raise suspicion of GERD. Proper diagnosis and treatment (i.e, hydrogen blockers, proton pump inhibitors, diet, elevating the head of the bed) not only can dramatically improve sleep but reduce the risk of esophageal erosion and dysplasia, which, if ignored, can increase the risk of esophageal cancer. One final note, research has established a link between sleep apnea and reflux. It seems to involve a mechanical or anatomic link between the lower esophageal sphincter and the phrenoesophageal ligament.[13] A bit technical, but significant. When sleep apnea is diagnosed, we should also look for GERD and *vice versa*.

Another classic GI culprit that disrupts sleep is peptic ulcer disease. One of the hallmark symptoms of a duodenal ulcer is waking up at 1:00 am or 2:00 am with epigastric pain. Sometimes the pain feels as if it radiates to the back. The pain of a duodenal ulcer is usually worse two or three hours after a meal and is often relieved by eating. Gastric ulcers (much less common) are characterized by pain immediately after eating. Elderly patients with peptic ulcer disease may have little or no pain until a catastrophic perforation occurs. The take-home message here is simple: any pain that awakens someone from a sound sleep is likely to be due to something significant. It should be taken seriously and worked up appropriately – in this case, with endoscopy.

Inflammatory bowel disease such as Crohn's or ulcerative colitis typically presents with multiple symptoms such as abdominal pain, distention, fever, weight loss, and diarrhea, often bloody. The point to keep in mind for our purpose is this: diarrhea due to inflammatory bowel disease often awakens the patient from a sound sleep. A recurring theme emerges. Symptoms due to stress, nervous tension, or anxiety can be troublesome throughout the day. But any symptom (i.e., chest pain, abdominal pain, cough, wheezing, or diarrhea) that awakens a person from deep sleep is usually something fairly serious.

A relatively common but under-recognized problem is splenic flexure syndrome. This is a mechanical or anatomic condition that can result in severe left upper quadrant abdominal pain. In some cases, the pain is so severe it mimics an MI. As the transverse colon transitions into the descending colon, it makes what amounts to a 90-degree turn or angle. When gas and/or stool gets trapped here, the colonic wall distends and intense pain can develop. In sedentary individuals (usually middle-aged or older), the symptoms intensify upon lying down. The next few hours can be brutal. A thorough physical examination (the old-fashioned kind with a stethoscope and abdominal percussion), along with an x-ray of the abdomen, can confirm the problem. The treatment involves regular activity, exercise, and avoiding gas-inducing foods.

Musculoskeletal Disorders that Disrupt Sleep

Most of us know first-hand that getting a good night's sleep when we're in pain is virtually impossible. Self-limited conditions like a muscle sprain, strain, or over-use injury, are frustrating enough.

Patients with Rheumatoid Arthritis have a high prevalence of restless legs syndrome.

If you do manage to get comfortable enough to fall asleep, you wake up easily and often upon changing positions in bed. The frustration mounts as painful conditions become chronic. We know that people with low back pain or arthritis are twice as likely to have trouble initiating or maintaining sleep as people without pain.[14] Arthritis is certainly one of the most common disorders that result in chronic pain. It's estimated that 60% of patients with arthritis endure pain at night. Osteoarthritis or degenerative joint disease tends to worsen as the day wears on, with pain often peaking in the evening. Rheumatoid arthritis (RA) pain tends to be most troublesome in the early morning. Typically, RA pain is accompanied by marked morning stiffness that lasts for an hour or more. Curiously, patients with RA have a high prevalence of restless legs syndrome (about 25%).[15]

Regardless of the type of arthritis, there is a definite relationship between pain and sleep, and it's not good. Pain results in poor sleep and poor sleep aggravates pain. The vicious cycle appears again. If you recall our discussion about sleep physiology and architecture, you recall that neurotransmitters like serotonin, norepinephrine, and dopamine are synthesized to a great extent during deep sleep. So is growth hormone. Night after night of uncomfortable tossing and turning depletes levels of these vital chemicals, increasing pain or at least the perception of it. Clinical evidence reveals that 31% of arthritis patients have trouble falling asleep, 81% have difficulty staying asleep, and about 50% tend to wake up too early in the morning.[16] Not surprisingly, poor sleep in people with arthritis correlates with greater perceived pain, decreased self-related health, poor functional status, and depression.[17] These folks are also most likely to try multiple types of self-care and pursue more medical treatments than similar patients without sleep disturbances.[18]

There is a definite relationship between pain and sleep, and it's not good.

These studies simply confirm what most of us have already figured out: when pain is at the root of insomnia, tossing sleeping pills at the patient will not do the trick. You have to relieve the pain. We've understood this for decades in the context of treating cancer patients. It's time to employ a little common sense in our efforts to help millions of people with insomnia and chronic, nonmalignant pain.

Chapter 5 - Medical Conditions That Disrupt Sleep

Diabetes & Sleep Disruption

Diabetes is one of the most common and challenging illnesses we deal with in clinical medicine. Every organ system in the body is affected to some degree. Cardiac, neurologic, renal, visual, vascular, and immune system complications are well described and anticipated. But diabetes can and typically does take a terrible toll on sleep. Disrupted sleep further aggravates the long list of diabetic complications.

The severity of diabetes and the extent to which it is controlled correlate directly with the severity of sleep disruption. Approximately one-third of people with diabetes experience significant sleep fragmentation.[19] Many factors contribute to this including paresthesias from peripheral neuropathy, leg cramps, restless legs syndrome, and periodic limb movements (both common in diabetes mellitus [DM]), nocturia, frequent urinary tract infections (UTI's), and cough.[20] Cough in diabetics may be due to frequent upper respiratory tract infections, congestive heart failure (CHF), sinusitis, allergies, and other conditions. Diabetics are actually at increased risk for obstructive sleep apnea, especially in the context of weight gain. Sleep deprivation in diabetics can exacerbate insulin resistance and worsen glucose control.[21] Any clinician who takes care of diabetic patients should routinely ask about sleep. Even a rigorous dietary program can only do so much if the patient is exhausted. The notion that diabetic control could be improved by regular, sound sleep is too important to be ignored. The pediatric implications alone are immense.

Renal Disease & Sleep Disruption

Chronic renal disease can be a serious complication of diabetes and hypertension, compromising the quality of life of hundreds of thousands of people. Well over half of patients with chronic renal disease report problems with sleep maintenance and early morning awakening. Many of these patients demonstrate marked abnormalities in their sleep electroencephalographys (EEG's), most of which are probably due to uremia and other metabolic aberrations.[22] Dialysis is associated with a number of sleep disorders including restless legs syndrome, periodic limb movements, obstructive sleep apnea, difficulty falling asleep, and excessive daytime somnolence.[23] Interestingly, obstructive sleep apnea often improves after dialysis is completed.[24] Most renal patients develop anemia or chronic disease at some point. This frequently worsens periodic limb movements. However, when their anemia is treated with erythropoietin, the number of limb movements decrease, and sleep quality improves.

The Prostate Gland & Sleep Disruption

Prostate problems are a major cause of insomnia in older men. The need to make multiple trips to the bathroom in the course of the night can exhaust the man himself and often his wife as well.

Benign prostatic hypertrophy (BPH) involves nonmalignant overgrowth of the prostate tissue that surrounds the urethra. The condition probably develops as a result of hormonal changes related to aging. Symptoms of BPH are familiar to many middle-aged and older men:

reduced stream, progressive urinary frequency and urgency, incomplete bladder emptying, and dribbling. Nocturia or nighttime voiding can occur three, four, or five times in the course of the night. Anything that disrupts sleep that frequently will compromise daytime well-being. Diagnosis of BPH is based on a digital rectal examination, cystoscopy, transrectal ultrasound, or urethrogram. None of these tests qualify as a leisure-time activity! And the reality is, many men avoid seeing a physician for this frustrating problem and end up suffering for years. Treatment with medications such as alpha-blockers and 5-alpha reductase inhibitors is helpful in most cases. In some cases, surgical intervention may be indicated. The downside is going to a doctor and enduring an unpleasant test or two. The upside is the possibility of sleeping through the night again (and not being tethered to a bathroom during the day).

Prostate problems are a major cause of insomnia in older men.

Dementia & Sleep Disruption

Most, if not all, of the dementing illnesses cause irreversible damage to areas of the brain that regulate sleep. Patients with Alzheimer's, vascular dementia, Lewy body dementia, Pick's disease, and Parkinson's experience profound changes in sleep architecture. Generally speaking, the more severe the dementia, the more severe the sleep disturbance.[25] In fact, in demented nursing home patients, not a single hour in a 24-hour period is spent fully awake or fully asleep.[26] Typically, these patients experience their greatest level of alertness during meals, but some patients will fall asleep even during a meal.

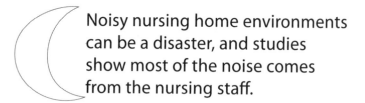

Noisy nursing home environments can be a disaster, and studies show most of the noise comes from the nursing staff.

Sleep studies in patients with dementia document difficulty initiating sleep, more sleep fragmentation, decreased total sleep time, and decreased slow-wave sleep.[27] Once again, the vicious cycle appears. Slow-wave sleep is vital for neurotransmitter synthesis (acetylcholine in the case of Alzheimer's). And inadequate neurotransmitter levels in dementia worsen sleep architecture. Although efforts to preserve and protect sleep in dementia patients will not cure or reverse the dementia, improved sleep does improve some aspects of behavior and cognition. If sleep disturbances are ignored in dementia patients, many problems will intensify: excessive daytime sleepiness, confusion, nighttime wandering, and sundowning (agitated behavior develops as ambient light levels decrease). Nighttime wandering and sundowning can quickly overwhelm the capacity of caregivers to cope. These two symptoms frequently precipitate the decision to place the patient in a nursing home. Most dementia patients are unable to articulate their sleeping problems, so caregivers and clinicians need to anticipate sleep disturbances and respond appropriately.

Treatment of sleep disorders in dementia patients is based on the nature or etiology of the problem. Continuous positive airway pressure (CPAP) can be used for sleep apnea and is actually tolerated better than we might expect. Restless legs syndrome and periodic limb movements respond fairly well to dopamine agonists. Some of the most practical strategies, however, include encouraging regular physical activity and exercise, exposure to sunlight early in the morning and late afternoon,[28] and regular social interaction to promote normal sleep/wake cycles. Noisy nursing home environments can be a disaster, and studies show most of the noise comes from the nursing staff.[29] There is no doubt that when noise is kept to a minimum and the environment is kept as dark as possible, sleep improves considerably. Avoiding daytime naps and caffeine can enhance both the quality and quantity of sleep in all age groups.

Anxiety & Sleep Disruption

We live in anxious times. Our frenetic, over-stimulated, over-extended lifestyles are clearly taking a toll on our peace of mind. A mere 25 years ago, no one was subjected to the neurosensory assault of cell phones, faxes, e-mail, or text messaging. Thirty years ago, we watched the evening news for a half hour or so and called it a day. Now we're bombarded by nearly every awful thing that happens anywhere in the world 24 hours a day, seven days a week. Our nervous systems are not sufficiently hard-wired to process constant negative stimuli without signaling distress – in many cases, that distress is expressed as anxiety.

> Anxiety disorders are diagnosed about twice as often in women as in men.

Significantly more research has been conducted on the relationship between depression and insomnia than on anxiety and insomnia. And yet, complaints regarding anxiety (or worry) and sleep disruption are very common in real world medical practice. Anxiety disorders are diagnosed about twice as often in women as in men, with generalized anxiety disorder (GAD) being recognized most often, and phobias coming in second.[30] Lower levels of income and education and poor quality housing are often associated with more anxiety. Chronic illness has long been known to exacerbate anxiety, especially in the elderly. Chronic lung disease, congestive heart failure, arrhythmias, hyperthyroidism, and adrenal gland tumors and disorders are among the classic culprits.[31,32,33]

A long list of medications can precipitate or aggravate anxious feelings, and here we find tremendous variation among individuals. Some common offenders include caffeine (in beverages and medications), theophylline, antihypertensives, anticholinergics, cold and flu remedies, and steroids. Every now and then a patient may have a paradoxical reaction to a medication intended to induce relaxation or sedation. The first time I observed this frightening phenomenon was years ago when I gave a patient a small dose of IV Ativan (lorazepam) before a procedure. Five minutes later he was practically climbing the walls. The opposite response will get your attention every time.

Dementing illnesses like Alzheimer's are often associated with anxiety. One study revealed as many as 71% of outpatients with Alzheimer's disease had an "anxious or worried appearance," and up to 57% displayed fidgeting, which may be a symptom of anxiety.[34] This is an important point. Sometimes what we perceive to be an agitated patient is really an anxious patient. Realizing this can have a huge impact on our treatment decisions.

> Dementing illnesses like Alzheimer's are often associated with anxiety.

Just as anxiety can disrupt sleep (delaying sleep onset and increasing fragmentation), insomnia can worsen anxiety. We've known for decades that people with severe insomnia experience more somatic symptoms of anxiety such as sweating, dizziness, jitteriness, and nervous stomach. Folks with insomnia also tend to have more anxiety, worry, and tension around bedtime, probably due to repeated conditioning. The best advice is simple: when patients complain of anxiety, we should evaluate them for insomnia, and *vice versa*.

Medications certainly may provide some benefit in the setting of anxiety and insomnia, but non-drug measures like exercise, relaxation techniques, meditation, counseling to deal with the root of the anxiety, and cognitive behavioral therapy are every bit as important.

Mental health professionals have a variety of screening tools they use to assess anxiety.

Some questions I've found helpful over the years are:

1. Do you often feel upset, jittery, or nervous?
2. Do you often feel threatened, anxious, or insecure?
3. Do you often worry about the past or the future?
4. Is it difficult for you to relax or unwind?
5. Are you frequently ill at ease?
6. Do you fret about things you can't control?
7. Does your heart race when you're worried?
8. Are your hands often cold or clammy?
9. Do you frequently have an upset stomach or a lump in your throat?
10. Do you feel tired all the time?
11. Does worry keep you awake at night?
12. Do you often dread facing tomorrow?

This is not a scientifically validated scale. But answering "yes" to more than three or four of these questions probably indicates the need for more formal evaluations.

Depression & Sleep Disruption

Depression is characterized by sadness severe enough to prevent normal daily function. Contributing factors include genetics, abnormal neurotransmitter levels, disrupted neuro-endocrine responses, environmental and psychosocial factors, other medical conditions, and even nutritional status. Sleep disruption is a classic symptom of depression and may involve insomnia, hypersomnia, fragmented sleep, or more often than not, early morning awakening.

> Depression is characterized by sadness severe enough to prevent normal daily function.

The typical scenario involves waking up at three or four o'clock in the morning and being unable to go back to sleep. This is also a common occurrence during menopause. So, it's very important to know the diagnostic criteria for depression. The presence of five or more of the following symptoms over two weeks or more is indicative of a major depression disorder:[35]

1. Persistent sad, anxious, blue, or empty mood.

2. Feelings of helplessness or pessimism.

3. Feelings of guilt, worthlessness, and hopelessness.

4. Loss of interest in pleasant activities or hobbies (inability to experience pleasure – anhedonia).

5. Decreased energy, fatigue, or being "slowed down."

6. Difficulty concentrating, remembering, or making decisions.

7. Insomnia, early morning awakening; hypersomnolence.

8. Changes in appetite or weight.

9. Suicidal thoughts or gestures.

10. Restlessness and irritability.

Despite the recent increased awareness about depression in the public arena and the medical profession, the role of sleep remains underappreciated. Nearly 90% of people with severe depression struggle with early morning insomnia.[36] In fact, depression actually affects sleep architecture. Sleep studies in depressed patients reveal less time spent in slow-wave (delta) sleep and a tendency to enter REM sleep more quickly early in the sleep cycle.

Insomnia is a very common complaint among depressed patients in primary care settings, and it may actually overshadow sadness as the chief complaint.

Repeat: depressed patients are often more troubled by insomnia than sadness! Understanding this key point is essential if we're to obtain a good history. Several well-tested tools are useful in clinical practice to assess depression. One of the most reliable is the Beck Depression Inventory.[37]

The Beck Depression Inventory

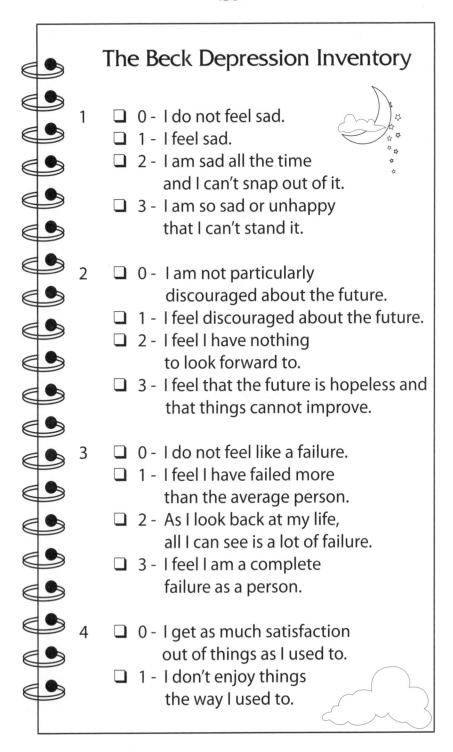

1
- ❑ 0 - I do not feel sad.
- ❑ 1 - I feel sad.
- ❑ 2 - I am sad all the time
  and I can't snap out of it.
- ❑ 3 - I am so sad or unhappy
  that I can't stand it.

2
- ❑ 0 - I am not particularly
  discouraged about the future.
- ❑ 1 - I feel discouraged about the future.
- ❑ 2 - I feel I have nothing
  to look forward to.
- ❑ 3 - I feel that the future is hopeless and
  that things cannot improve.

3
- ❑ 0 - I do not feel like a failure.
- ❑ 1 - I feel I have failed more
  than the average person.
- ❑ 2 - As I look back at my life,
  all I can see is a lot of failure.
- ❑ 3 - I feel I am a complete
  failure as a person.

4
- ❑ 0 - I get as much satisfaction
  out of things as I used to.
- ❑ 1 - I don't enjoy things
  the way I used to.

❑ 2 - I don't get any real satisfaction
out of anything anymore.
❑ 3 - I am dissatisfied or
bored with everything.

5 ❑ 0 - I don't feel particularly guilty.
❑ 1 - I feel guilty a good part of the time.
❑ 2 - I feel quite guilty most of the time.
❑ 3 - I feel guilty all of the time.

6 ❑ 0 - I don't feel as if I'm being punished.
❑ 1 - I feel I may be punished.
❑ 2 - I expect to be punished.
❑ 3 - I feel I am being punished.

7 ❑ 0 - I don't feel disappointed in myself.
❑ 1 - I am disappointed in myself.
❑ 2 - I am disgusted with myself.
❑ 3 - I hate myself.

8 ❑ 0 - I don't feel I am any
worse than anybody else.
❑ 1- I am critical of myself for
my weakness or mistakes.
❑ 2 - I blame myself all
the time for my faults.
❑ 3 - I blame myself for everything bad
that happens.

9
- ❑ 0 - I don't have any
thoughts of killing myself.
- ❑ 1 - I have thoughts of killing myself,
but I would not carry them out.
- ❑ 2 - I would like to kill myself.
- ❑ 3 - I would kill myself
if I had the chance.

10
- ❑ 0 - I don't cry any more than usual.
- ❑ 1 - I cry more now than I used to.
- ❑ 2 - I cry all the time now.
- ❑ 3 - I used to be able to cry, but now
I can't cry even though I want to.

11
- ❑ 0 - I am no more irritated
by things than I ever am.
- ❑ 1 - I am slightly more
irritated now than usual.
- ❑ 2 - I am quite annoyed or
irritated a good deal of the time.
- ❑ 3 - I feel irritated all the time now.

12
- ❑ 0 - I have not lost
interest in other people.
- ❑ 1- I am less interested in
other people than I used to be.
- ❑ 2 - I have lost most of my
interest in other people.
- ❑ 3 - I have lost all my interest
in other people.

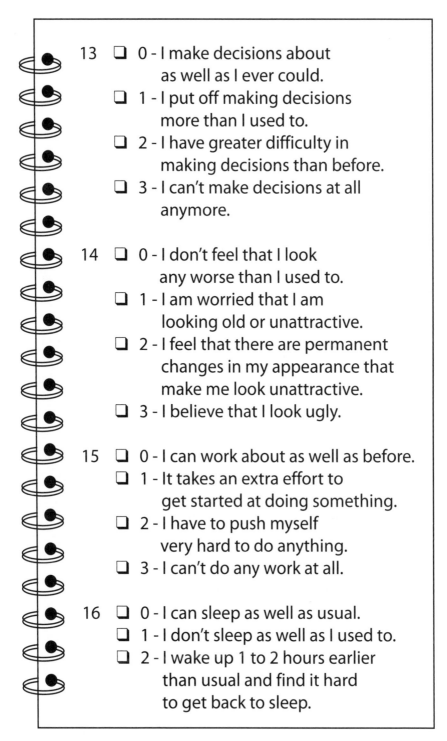

13 ☐ 0 - I make decisions about
      as well as I ever could.
   ☐ 1 - I put off making decisions
      more than I used to.
   ☐ 2 - I have greater difficulty in
      making decisions than before.
   ☐ 3 - I can't make decisions at all
      anymore.

14 ☐ 0 - I don't feel that I look
      any worse than I used to.
   ☐ 1 - I am worried that I am
      looking old or unattractive.
   ☐ 2 - I feel that there are permanent
      changes in my appearance that
      make me look unattractive.
   ☐ 3 - I believe that I look ugly.

15 ☐ 0 - I can work about as well as before.
   ☐ 1 - It takes an extra effort to
      get started at doing something.
   ☐ 2 - I have to push myself
      very hard to do anything.
   ☐ 3 - I can't do any work at all.

16 ☐ 0 - I can sleep as well as usual.
   ☐ 1 - I don't sleep as well as I used to.
   ☐ 2 - I wake up 1 to 2 hours earlier
      than usual and find it hard
      to get back to sleep.

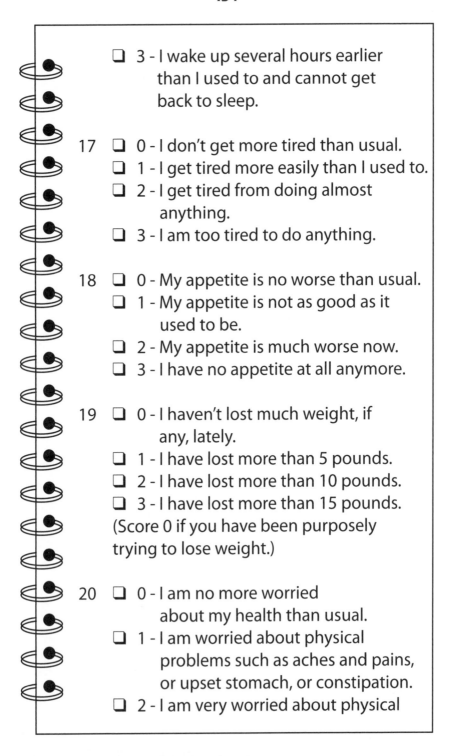

❏ 3 - I wake up several hours earlier than I used to and cannot get back to sleep.

17 ❏ 0 - I don't get more tired than usual.
❏ 1 - I get tired more easily than I used to.
❏ 2 - I get tired from doing almost anything.
❏ 3 - I am too tired to do anything.

18 ❏ 0 - My appetite is no worse than usual.
❏ 1 - My appetite is not as good as it used to be.
❏ 2 - My appetite is much worse now.
❏ 3 - I have no appetite at all anymore.

19 ❏ 0 - I haven't lost much weight, if any, lately.
❏ 1 - I have lost more than 5 pounds.
❏ 2 - I have lost more than 10 pounds.
❏ 3 - I have lost more than 15 pounds.
(Score 0 if you have been purposely trying to lose weight.)

20 ❏ 0 - I am no more worried about my health than usual.
❏ 1 - I am worried about physical problems such as aches and pains, or upset stomach, or constipation.
❏ 2 - I am very worried about physical

problems, and it's hard to think
of much else.

❏ 3 - I am so worried about my physical
problems that I cannot think
about anything else.

21 ❏ 0 - I have not noticed any recent
change in my interest in sex.

❏ 1 - I am less interested in sex than
I used to be.

❏ 2 - I am much less interested in
sex now.

❏ 3 - I have lost interest in sex
completely.

Total Score

❏   01-10 These ups and downs
are considered normal

❏   11-16 Mild mood disturbance

❏   17-20 Borderline clinical
depression

❏   21-30 Moderate depression

❏   31-40 Severe depression

❏   >40   Extreme depression

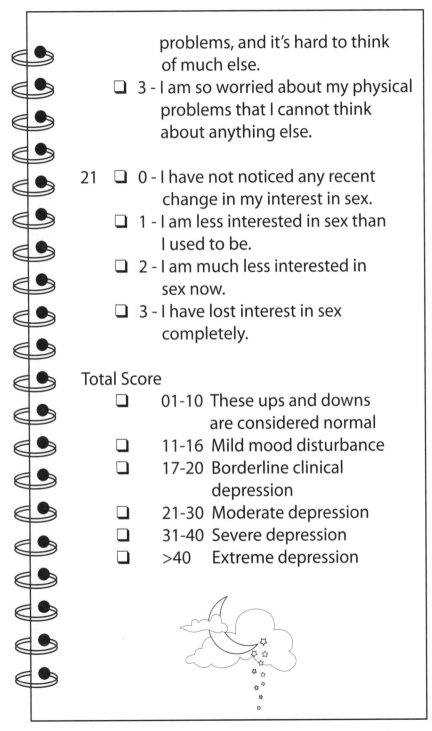

If depression is the likely cause of insomnia, an appropriately selected antidepressant or combination of antidepressants may help both the insomnia and depression. Best results are always obtained with a comprehensive treatment strategy that includes counseling, cognitive behavioral therapy, exercise, good nutrition, a more uplifting, pleasant environment, and, for many people, attention to spiritual matters.

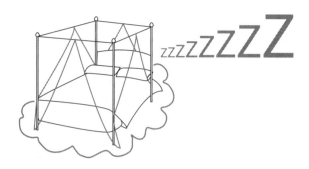

References

1. Foley D, Ancoli-Israel S, Britz P, Walsh J. Sleep disturbances and chronic disease in older adults: Results of the 2003 National Sleep Foundation Sleep in America Survey. *J Psychosom Res* 2004;56:497-502.

2. National Institutes of Health. State-of-the-Science. Conference Statement on Manifestations and Management of Chronic Insomnia in Adults. *Sleep.*2005;28(9):1049-1057.

3. McCracken LM, Iverson GL. Disrupted sleep patterns and daily functioning in patients with chronic pain. *Pain Res Manag.* 2002;7: 75-79.

4. Savard J, Morin CM. Insomnia in the context of cancer: A review of a neglected problem. *J Clin Oncol.* 2001;19: 895-908.

5. Fleetham J, West P. Mezon B, et al. Sleep, arousals, and oxygen desaturations in chronic obstructive pulmonary disorder: The effect of oxygen therapy. *Am Rev Respir Dis.* 1982;126: 429-433.

6. Martin RJ, Bartelson BL, Smith P, et al. Effect of ipratropium bromide treatment in oxygen saturation and sleep quality in COPD. *Chest* 1999;115:1338-1345.

7. Mallon L, Broman JE, Hett J. Sleep complaints predict coronary artery disease mortality in males: A 12-year follow-up study of a middle-aged Swedish population. *J Int Med.* 2002; 251: 207-216.

8. Ingber M, Freemark D. Adler Y. Cheyne-Stokes breathing disorder in patients with congestive heart failure: Incidence, pathophysiology, treatment and prognosis. [Hebrew] *Harefuah.* 2001;140:1209-1212.

9. Lanfranchi PA, Braghiroli A, Bosimini E, et al. Prognostic value of nocturnal Cheyne-Stokes respiration in chronic heart failure. *Circulation.* 1999;99:1435-1440.

10. Quaranta AJ, D'Alonzo GE, Krachman SL. Cheyne-Stokes respiration during sleep in congestive heart failure. *Chest* 1997; 111(2): 467-473.

11. Chocron S, Tatou E, Schjoth B, et al. Perceived health status in patients over 70 before and after open-heart operations. *Age Aging.* 2000;29: 329-334.

12. Orr WC. Sleep and gastroesophageal reflux disease: A wake-up call. *Rev Gastroenterol Disord.* 2004;4(Suppl 4): 525-532.

13. Herr, J. Chronic cough, sleep apnea, and gastroesophgeal reflux disease. *Chest.* 2001;120:1036-1037.

14. Gislason T, Almiquist M. Somatic diseases and sleep complaints. An epidemiological study of 3,201 Swedish men. *Acta Med Scan.* 1987;221(5):475-481.

15. Ondo W, Tan EK, Mansoor J. Rheumatologic serologies in secondary restless legs syndrome. *Mov Disord.* 2000;15:321-323.

16. Wilcox S, Brenes GA, Levine D, et al. Factors related to sleep disturbance in older adults experiencing knee pain or knee pain with radiographic evidence of knee osteoarthritis. *J Am Geriatr Soc.* 2000;48:1241-1251.

17. Jordan JM, Bernhard SL, Callahan LF, et al. Self-reported arthritis-related disruption in sleep and daily life and the use of medical, complementary, and self-care strategies for arthritis. *Arch Fam Med.* 2000;9:143-149.

18. Sridhar GR, Madhu K. Prevalence of sleep disturbances in diabetes mellitus. *Diabetes Res Clin Pract.* 1994;23:183-186.

19. Lammond N, Tiggemann M, Dawson D. Factors predicting sleep disruption in Type II diabetes. *Sleep.* 2000;23:415-416.

20. Van Cauter E, Polonsky KS, Sheen AJ. Roles of circadian rhythmicity and sleep in human glucose regulation. *Endocr Rev.* 1997;18:716-738.

21. Williams SW, Tell GS, Zheng B, et al. Correlate of sleep behavior among hemodialysis patients: The Kidney Outcomes Prediction and Evaluation (KOPE) study. *Am J Nephrol.* 2002;22:18-28.

22. Parker KP. Sleep disturbance in dialysis patients. *Sleep Med Rev.* 2003;7:131-143.

23. Hanly PJ, Pierratos A. Improvement of sleep apnea in patients with chronic renal failure who undergo nocturnal hemodialysis. *N Eng J Med.* 2001;344:102-107.

24. Pat-Horenczyk R, Klauber MR, Shochat T, Ancoli-Israel S. Hourly profiles of sleep and wakefulness in severely versus mild-moderately demented nursing home patients. *Aging Clin Exp Res.* 1998;10: 308-315.

25. Vitiello MV. Sleep disorders and aging. *Curr Opin Psychiatry.* 1996;9(4): 284-289.

26. Ancoli-Israel S, Gehrman P, Martin JL, et al. Increased light exposure consolidates sleep and strengthens circadian rhythms in severe Alzheimer's disease patients. *Behav Sleep Med.* 2003;1:22-36.

27. Schonelle JF, Ouslander JG, Simmons SF, et al. The nighttime environment, incontinence care, and sleep disruption in nursing homes. *J Am Geriatr Soc.* 1993;41(9): 910-914.

28. Beekman AT, Bremmer MA, Deeg DJ, et al. Anxiety disorders in later life: A report from the Longitudinal Aging Study Amsterdam. *Int J Geriatr Psychiatry.* 1998;13(10): 717-726.

29. Barnett M. Chronic obstructive pulmonary disease: A phenomenological study of patients' experiences. *J Clin Nursing.* 2005;14(7): 805-812.

30. Periyakoil VS, Skultety K, Sheikh J. Panic, anxiety, and chronic dyspnea. *J Palliat Med.* 2005;8(2):453-459.

31. Sait Gonen M, Kisakol G, Savas Cilli A, et al. Assessment of anxiety in subclinical thyroid disorders. *Endocr J.* 2004;51(3): 311-315.

32. Fervertti L, McCurry SM, Logsdon R, et al. Anxiety and Alzheimer's disease. *J Geriatric Psychiatry Neurol.* 2001:14(1):52-58.

33. American Psychiatric Association. *Diagnostic and Statistical Manual of Mental Disorders: DSM-IV.* 4th ed. Washington, DC. American Psychiatric Press. 1994: 551-607.

34. McCall WV, Reboussin BA, Cohen W. Subjective measurement of insomnia and quality of life in depressed inpatients. *J Sleep Res.* 2000; 91(1):43-48.

35. Beck AT, Ward CH, Mendelson M, et al. An inventory for measuring depression. *Arch Gen Psychiatry.* 1961;4: 561-571.

Chapter **6**

Exhaustion in the 21st Century

(Or how to get a really terrible night's sleep)

"Have courage for the great sorrows of life and patience for the small ones; and when you have laboriously accomplished your daily task, go to sleep in peace. God is awake."

—Victor Hugo
French dramatist, novelist, & poet
(1802 - 1885)

Who among us is not exhausted much of the time? As I travel across the country lecturing, I hear a streaming litany of complaints, "I am so tired," "I'm just fried," "I can't remember the last time I had a good night's sleep." From ages 18 to 88, people are run down, worn out, and frustrated. Not all of us can blame acute or chronic illness for our insomnia. Bad habits can creep into anyone's lifestyle and wreak havoc with sleep architecture. Could it be that one or more of these culprits have infiltrated your life?

Ten Common Unhealthy Habits

1. Inactivity

Have you ever been mentally or emotionally drained but not physically tired enough to sleep? Many of us experience this situation on a regular basis. Despite the fact that we work long hours (12-hour shifts are now commonplace), human beings were not designed to sit at a desk all day, or stand behind a pharmacy counter, or stare at a computer screen. We were designed to walk and move. Perhaps, on occasion, you've experienced the "good kind of tired" that comes from hours of working in the garden or having a refreshing swim or a couple of hours of ballroom dancing (I vote for that one!). Those activities confer a considerable list of benefits.

1. They build muscle strength.

2. They enhance joint flexibility.

3. They promote coordination and balance.

4. They foster a sense of accomplishment.

5. They help relieve stress and dissipate negative energy.

6. They enhance endorphin production.

7. They reduce cortisol levels.

8. They increase stamina and endurance.

9. They reduce the severity of menstrual cramps and hot flashes.

10. They burn calories and facilitate weight loss.

11. They help stabilize sleep architecture.

12. They induce a pleasurable state known as fun.

In fact, there is even evidence now that regular exercise increases the volume of grey and white matter in the brain!

If someone could develop a medication that provided that many benefits, she could retire a billionaire tomorrow.

The challenge here, of course, is classic. When you're sleep-deprived and exhausted, the last thing you feel like doing is, well, the "E word," or exercise.

Most of us in health care have had the experience of advising a patient, "Sir, you really need to get more exercise into your routine." And people will roll their eyes and scrunch up their noses and recite a litany of all the reasons they could not possibly exercise. "Oh, but you don't understand. My feet hurt, my ankles are weak, my knees ache, I get short of breath, and we don't have sidewalks." I've heard the sidewalk excuse for 30 years. But the most popular excuse of all is the ever reliable "I don't have time!" Pretty silly. We all have precisely the same amount of time each day. Do you know someone who gets 26 hours in her day? People make time for things that really matter to them. Isn't it curious that every President since John F. Kennedy has made time for exercise in her daily routine? Presidential schedules and responsibilities far exceed anything the rest of us contend with. If they manage to make time for the "E word," we have no excuses! If none of this has convinced you of the need to banish inactivity in your pursuit of sleep, just try it. Make the effort to get off your gluteus maximus every day for three weeks. If you don't notice better quality sleep, more strength, more stamina, a slimmer waistline, and a better mood, you can always go back to being a tired, grumpy slug!

2. Overeating & Indigestion

This is starting to read like a weight loss book. That's okay. Weight loss often improves sleep quality. Overeating, abdominal bloating and distention, dyspepsia, indigestion, gas pains, and gastro-esophageal reflux are more than capable of preventing or interrupting sleep. Gastrointestinal (GI) problems seem to be more widespread than ever, and much of the blame falls in the lap of lifestyle. Our lifestyles have changed radically since World War II. Consider the way our grandparents and great grandparents used to eat. Long, long ago, in a galaxy far, far away, women were known to get up and "cook" breakfast. And what did they cook for breakfast? Oatmeal, ham and eggs, and biscuits, etc. Food was properly viewed as fuel for a physically demanding day. A snack was an apple or a handful of nuts. Lunch, or "noontime dinner" was the big meal of the day, with the chicken and the mashed potatoes and the green beans and the apple pie. Supper was much lighter fare – homemade bread and soup. And after supper, people didn't sit around watching sitcoms and reality shows. They lived reality. They didn't need to watch it on television (which didn't exist).

Women continued their endless list of strenuous chores and men worked out in the vegetable garden and did their own yard work. No one was standing in front of the refrigerator with the door wide open at 11:00 pm waiting to have a religious experience. By that time they were ready to collapse into bed. Seventy or eighty years ago, people weren't stuffing their faces with pizzas and fast food and soda pop and assorted other forms of junk. Today, millions of people sleep till the very last minute (because they're so sleep deprived), race through the shower, toss on some clothes, and head to work or school without breakfast. At some point they're apt to indulge in a super-sized giant mocha-cocoa-loco latte. Many of these drinks contain enough sugar, fat, and caffeine to sink a ship. Lunch, in many cases, is a totally underwhelming event consisting of salad or more fast food. By 4:30 pm or 5:00 pm most of us would kill for a Snicker's bar or a hot fudge sundae or both. In far too many cases, we eat dinner out in some restaurant where we're presented with enough food for a week. Do we stop there? No. We continue to munch away as we sit in front of our bright, over-stimulating, big screen televisions. And we wonder why we have record-breaking sales of Maalox, Mylanta, Zantac, Nexium, Pepcid, Pepcid AC, Pepcid Complete, Pepcid Forever, and Pepcid Amen.

It makes no sense to eat the bulk of our calories toward the end of the day. It's not good for our waistlines and it certainly won't induce sound slumber.

What should we be doing? Eat a healthy breakfast. Minimize junk food. Lighten up on fats – especially later in the day. Reduce portions. Eliminate foods that provoke symptoms of gas or indigestion. Have a small light snack (a couple of graham crackers, a custard cup full of cereal) about 90 minutes before bedtime. If GI (gastro-intestinal) symptoms persist, see a physician. Chances are good he or she will give you exactly the same advice.

3. Overstimulation

Are you uptight, stressed out and overstimulated? If the answer to that question is "no," please share your secret with the rest of us. As a physician I have my share of 18- and 20-hour days. But work, *per se*, is not what wears me out. What wears me out is noise and chaos. If you've been in an airport lately, you know whereof I speak. Everywhere you turn, you find yourself bombarded by uncivilized levels of noise. Loud, rude people with their loud, rude contraptions infiltrate every square foot. Even the bathrooms and business lounges reverberate with ill-mannered, obstreperous people. Remember hearing your grandmother say, "There's a time and a place for everything"? I think we need a giant, global reminder. Have you found yourself in a restroom recently? And you realize that the mental giant in the stall next to you is having a cell phone conversation while she is going to the bathroom?

Someday I am going to blurt out what I've been thinking for years, "Were you raised by wolves?" Do you know people who can't get through the grocery store without three or four incredibly trite cell phone conversations? Add everyone's incessant prattle to blaring televisions, radios, buzzers, beepers, and overhead announcements, and you can no longer hear yourself think. But wait! We haven't even mentioned computers, laptops, Blackberries, DVD players, iPods, and assorted other electronic gadgets. Walk into any home, hospital, pharmacy, office, store, or shop, and your senses will, in all likelihood, be assaulted. Malignant overstimulation has even metastasized to churches. Not long ago I popped in to my neighborhood church after services were over to have a little thinking time. I'd like to say I was there because I'm so holy and enlightened, but the truth is, I just wanted some peace and quiet. Unfortunately, there was none to be found. Peace and quiet, that is. Fussy, noisy chatterboxes were milling about mindlessly. Somehow the notion that a church should be a place of quiet, reverent reflection escaped them.

What does any of this have to do with sleep? Simple.

Areas of the brain that regulate sleep don't turn on and off like a switch. Few of us can go through an 18-hour day with overstimulated senses and raw, frayed nerves and then slide into sound slumber. The fact that we've been up to our eyeballs in technology over the last 20 years doesn't mean that our nervous systems have adapted. Constant overcrowding and congestion don't help either. No matter how slick and sophisticated we become, human beings will always need a certain amount of solitude, peace, and quiet.

4. Excessive Worry

When overstimulation is a problem, excessive worry is usually not far behind. Human beings have always had their own personal concerns and worries, chief among them over the millennia has been survival. Sound sleep presumes a certain level of safety and security. Whenever we feel threatened or endangered, multiple regions in the brain kick in to maintain or heighten alertness. Active thought keeps the frontal lobes in high gear; fear and anxiety jump start the limbic system and amygdalae; stress and worry irritate the reticular activating system. Before you know it, the hypothalamus is having a discussion with the pituitary gland, the pituitary gland has a conversation with the adrenal glands, and boom! Adrenaline levels surge, soon to be followed by a spike in a cortisol production. All of this worked really well tens of thousands of years ago if you heard a saber-tooth tiger growling just outside your cave. The resulting physiologic changes enabled you to run like crazy or fight like the dickens, either of which is handy if survival is the goal. Today, however, our worries encompass more numerous and nefarious dangers than wild animals outside the cave. We have all the usual concerns simmering along our synapses: personal health; health and well-being of children, spouses, parents and friends; financial issues; problems at work; taxes; traffic; and wild weather. Our own problems are more than enough to keep us wide awake at night. But now our high-tech culture imposes the problems of the world upon us. Remember how difficult it was to sleep in the weeks right after 9/11? We were numb from seeing horrific images played over and over. In the years since, we've lived with the lingering worry that something equally awful might happen again.

The truth is, we watch awful events occurring all over the world every day on the news: car bombings, kidnappings, war, hurricanes, tsunamis, earthquakes, tornadoes, and the heartbreaking human suffering that results. How could thinking people not worry – for themselves, their loved ones, or their fellow human beings? But, neurologically speaking, we're not really hard-wired to handle all the woes of the world. Our nervous systems have developed or evolved to handle threats in our own environment. Think about it, 70 or 80 years ago, someone in Indiana would never have heard about an earthquake in Indonesia, much less see endless images of the resulting devastation. Take it back several hundred years, or even several thousand years, and our dilemma becomes clear. So how can any thoughtful, concerned, sensitive person ever get a decent night's sleep knowing about the problems of millions? Despite having read a vast number of articles on the subject of anxiety or worry, the very best approach I've encountered so far has nothing to do with neurology or pharmacology. It has to do with an old-fashioned prayer: God grant me the serenity to accept the things I cannot change, the courage to change the things I can, and the wisdom to know the difference. That is some fine spiritual teaching. But speaking as a doctor, that's some superb psychology!

5. Erratic Schedules

If you hate sleep, may I recommend you adopt a really erratic schedule? That, of course, is precisely what many of us have done in recent years. Remember being a little kid and seeing your dad go off to work as you got ready for school? And, if you're a baby boomer or older, your mom supervised everyone? Then, after school, you had a snack, chores, and homework. Many of us were then expected to set the table and – I know this is a shocker – sit down to dinner with the whole family – nearly every night! Perhaps in the fall of 2007 you saw the television ads for "National Family Dinner Night." When the family dinner hour has become so rare that we need television ads to remind us of it, we have a problem. It's a symptom of our collective lifestyle. We sleep in until the last second (because we're so sleep deprived); we race to school or work, inhale junk for lunch; drag ourselves home long enough for a pit stop before racing back out to endless extracurricular activities, meetings, practice sessions, and social events. Then we vegetate in front of the television before we toss and turn in bed. Weekends are anyone's guess, but they're usually not very predictable or relaxing. But perhaps you're old enough to remember when they were – predictable and relaxing. For years, in my family, Sunday was a ritual: go to church, have a nice family breakfast, clean up the kitchen, read the Sunday paper, help outside with yard work, get cleaned up, eat a nice Sunday supper, and watch the "Wonderful World of Disney." It was like clockwork. It was far from exciting, but the familiarity of the routine was reassuring and comforting. Sleep came easily on Sunday nights despite anticipation of Monday morning. During stressful times, a stable routine can be a source of solace. It's cheap. It's safe. And it doesn't require a prescription. But don't let me influence you. If you love exhaustion, just maintain an insanely erratic schedule (like the one you probably have now).

6. Overextension

If you're dealing with overstimulation, excessive worry and a crazy schedule, there is a very good chance you're overextended. It's tough to sleep well when you feel as if you're being pulled in a hundred different directions. Unfortunately, most of us believe we're supposed to be overextended if we're hard working and successful. But that's not true. Juggling too many things at once (otherwise known as multi-tasking) is a great way to do many things poorly. Details are overlooked, important issues are neglected, mistakes are made, and stress levels surge. Next thing you know, tossing and turning all night long becomes a way of life.

We need to understand that hard work and overextension are not synonyms. Since the dawn of civilization through biblical times and the Middles Ages hard work was essential for survival. During the depression our grandparents and great-grandparents had to work hard to keep a roof over their heads and simple food on the table. But most of them had little trouble sleeping. Our situation is different. Even though many of us work hard, much of our energy is squandered on unnecessary activities. Take meetings, for example. There are corporate, medical, professional, social, neighborhood, or church-related meetings. If half of them were suddenly eliminated, it's unlikely your family would starve. What about after-school activities? What child truly needs to play on three different teams plus cheerleading, band practice, and drama club? One or two of those endeavors would be fine. But today, even our kids are overextended. We've convinced ourselves all this is necessary if they're to get into a good college. Not so. Focused excellence is always preferable to shotgun mediocrity. Besides, overextended, exhausted parents plus overextended, exhausted kids equals major league tension at home.

The solution is fairly simple (although we do handstands to pretend it's impossible). De-clutter your life. You may want to start with your closets and work your way up to your calendar. De-cluttering demands on your time requires frequent recitation of the word, "No." Assorted people will become upset. They'll get over it.

7. Caffeine, Nicotine & Alcohol

Do I even need to say it? If you're overstimulated, worried, overextended, and struggling with an erratic schedule, you may be tempted to consume too much of these culprits.

This, of course, is not a good idea unless you enjoy sleep disruption and deprivation.

Technically speaking, caffeine is probably the most widely used drug on the planet. This ubiquitous substance finds its way into our bodies courtesy of coffee; tea; colas; over-the-counter medications for headaches, colds, appetite suppressants; and (you didn't hear this from me) chocolate. Actually, the caffeine content in cocoa or chocolate is fairly modest unless you're really overdoing it.

People vary widely in their sensitivity to the stimulant effects of caffeine. But there is no doubt that caffeine can increase pulse rate and blood pressure, increase alertness, reduce fatigue (temporarily, at least), and even affect brain wave patterns. These physiologic effects can kick in within 15 to 20 minutes and last for five, six, or seven hours. The metabolism of caffeine or its half-life (how long it hangs around in your body) is influenced by age, hormone levels, pregnancy, smoking, and a variety of medical conditions. Even under the most simple, straightforward clinical conditions, if someone uses coffee or soda to combat late afternoon or early evening fatigue, insomnia may creep into the picture that night. There are certainly individuals who have a natural tolerance for caffeine. They can drink two or three cups of coffee in the evening and still fall fast asleep. However, they are probably not reading this book.

Caffeine can also cause a few troublesome daytime symptoms: nervousness, shakiness, and, ever popular in the workplace, irritability. Consuming large quantities of caffeine (over 500 mg/day) can foster dependency and withdrawal symptoms, including headaches, insomnia, and anxiety. Today, lots of folks are ingesting more caffeine than they realize. The standard 7-ounce cup of coffee people used to know and love has, in many cases, been replaced by the 12-ounce wonder. Drinking three of these oversized coffees can easily boost you over the 500 mg range. Cream and sugar with that cup of insomnia?

It's important to note that caffeine can also act as a mild diuretic. Combined with the effect of drinking additional fluid, consuming coffee in the evening can disrupt sleep by causing nocturia. Nighttime trips to the bathroom can interfere with everyone's sleep in the whole household. Drinking hot tea or cocoa in the evening can have a similar effect, but with these beverages, fluid volume is usually a bigger culprit than caffeine content. The best advice is to avoid caffeine within seven hours of bedtime. People who are sensitive to caffeine or really struggling with insomnia should avoid it after lunchtime or gradually eliminate caffeine completely. A word of caution: don't stop caffeine abruptly. The headache induced by caffeine withdrawal is nasty. Taper off slowly! Expect to sleep better.

Smoking cigarettes is a very effective way to shorten your life. In the United States, smoking contributes to over 400,000 deaths each year: cancer of the mouth, lips, tongue, esophagus, stomach, colon, kidneys, lungs, breast, cervix, just to name a few malignancies; plus transient ischemic attack (TIA); stroke; myocardial infarction (MI); deep venous thrombosis; pulmonary embolism; asthma; emphysema; and pneumonia. Most people know this, even if they try hard to stay in denial. But not everyone understands how disruptive nicotine is when it comes to sleep. Nicotine is a stimulant with symptoms reminiscent of caffeine – increased pulse, blood pressure, respiratory rate, adrenaline production, and even faster brain wave activity. These effects can linger for several hours after the last cigarette, which can make falling asleep and staying asleep a challenge.

But wait! There's more. Nicotine withdrawal can begin within a few hours of the last cigarette (even less time in a heavy smoker). Restlessness, irritability, anxiety, headaches, lighter sleep, and frequent awakenings can make nights miserable. Smoking also irritates mucosal surfaces in the nasal passages and pharynx. Translation: more snoring. It's a rare individual who can smoke cigarettes and truly have a great night's sleep. The best bet is to stop smoking, preferably "cold turkey." (Most people who manage to stop smoking permanently use the "cold turkey" approach.) You'll sleep better. And in all likelihood, you'll live longer. Probably a lot longer.

What about a nightcap? Don't even think about it. Physicians over the years have actually written standing orders for hospital or nursing home patients to have a bedtime drink to help them fall asleep (the patient, not the doctor). Here's the problem: even though a cocktail or a glass of wine may help you relax and fall asleep more easily, it can fragment or disrupt sleep a few hours later, leaving you wide awake. Alcohol can suppress dream sleep and stimulate the reticular activating system of the brainstem. As the night progresses and the alcohol is metabolized, rebound rapid eye movement (REM) sleep can occur, resulting in unpleasant and intense dreams or nightmares. Mild alcohol withdrawal can develop by early morning, say between 2:00 am and 3:00 am, thus further disrupting sleep. Alcohol is certainly capable of relaxing muscles, including muscles in the pharynx. This exacerbates snoring and can easily aggravate sleep apnea. Most of this is not a problem if you're 20 years old. But as we age, we tend to become more sensitive to the effects of alcohol on sleep architecture. There's nothing wrong with an occasional cocktail or glass of wine. But if you're not sleeping well, pay attention to how your body is really reacting to that drink. You may not be relaxing quite as much as you think.

8. Bedroom Blunders

I can think of eight: temperature, light, noise, clutter, pets, bed, space, and spouse, but not necessarily in that order.

Let's tackle one at a time.

Temperature – Being too hot or too cold can interfere with anyone's sleep. But more often than not, waking up overheated and clammy is the culprit. Hot flashes or night sweats can be problematic in menopause or even peri-menopause (which, by the way, can drag on for 8 or 10 years beginning in your late 30s or early 40s). But even babies can wake up hot, sweaty, and cranky. No one's body temperature remains perfectly static through the night. Toss in overly heavy blankets or comforters and a less than perfect heating or cooling system and a miserable night may be on the way. Believe it or not, there is an optimal temperature for sleep – and we'll discuss it in Chapter Eight.

Light – Have you ever found yourself wide awake in the middle of the night courtesy of a streetlight shining through a crack in the drapes or even the moon at just the right angle? If you're really sensitive to light (and many women are) the offending light source can be as small as an alarm clock with a luminescent dial, a nightlight in the hallway or bathroom, or an old VCR still flashing "12:00." If you still have an old VCR flashing "12:00," it's time to upgrade. One of the most pervasive villains in this arena is the flickering images on your television screens. Even if the volume is turned down, the flickering images on the television can irritate the reticular activating system in the brain and fragment sleep. Do not, repeat, do not fall asleep with the television on – unless you actually enjoy exhaustion.

Noise – In terms of sleep disruption, noise is right up there with light. A hundred years ago, the main source of noise in the evening was the sound of crickets and conversation. Today most households reverberate with the cacophony of multiple televisions, radios, DVD's, video games, various phones, and even assorted office equipment. And that doesn't even include the kids, spouse, pets, neighbors, traffic, weather-related sounds, and outdoor critters. I have a cathedral ceiling in my bedroom, which is a lovely design feature. Unfortunately, a family of raccoons considers it the perfect playground. At three o'clock in the morning, the noise engendered by four racoons bears a remarkable auditory similarity to a herd of stampeding buffalo. However, as annoying as that sound is, it's downright melodic compared to the screeching, rumbling roar of 300,000 motorcycles invading town for biker week rallies several times a year. Perhaps you must contend with comparable noises at night. I have one word: earplugs.

Clutter – Have you ever taken a good hard look at your bedroom? Is it a disaster zone? Are there piles of magazines, catalogs, journals and books? Is there a piece of exercise equipment that has turned into an expensive clothes rack? Are shoes, boots, and slippers scattered on the floor? Can you actually see the floor? Perhaps you have more sophisticated clutter. Perhaps your clutter is mostly work-related. Unless I'm constantly policing myself, my bedroom can start to look like the local branch of a medical library. This is not conducive to sleep. To my knowledge, there are no long-term randomized, double-blind, placebo-controlled studies on the effects of clutter on sleep architecture. However, from a purely psychological perspective, clutter is not good. Proponents of feng shui would explain that clutter blocks good energy flow.

Medical science isn't quite ready to back up that belief, but climbing over clutter on your way to bed won't help. When in doubt, de-clutter!

Pets – Don't hate me here! I like animals. But having Fluffy, Fido, or Fifi in your bed is not a good idea if the goal is uninterrupted sleep. If your furry friend has slept by your side for years and you sleep like a log, skip ahead to the next book. It is important to understand that pets can disturb your sleep on several levels: jumping on and off the bed, making assorted noises, restricting your natural movement during sleep, and aggravating allergies you may not even realize you have. Unfortunately, people can be very stubborn. Speaking as a doctor, I can't think of any single habit people cling to more than this one. If any of this rings a bell, please don't be stubborn. You'll be better able to care for your pet if you're healthy, and it's tough to stay healthy for long without adequate sleep.

Bed – Are you still sleeping on the same mattress you got when you were married back in 1973? Time for a new one! An

Upgrading your bedding is one of the simplest ways to improve sleep quality.

uncomfortable bed and pitiful pillows are common culprits in the realm of sleep deprivation. Neck, back, or hip pain from inadequate support can make nights and mornings miserable. Synthetic fibers in sheets and pillowcases can contribute to overheating in the middle of the night. Upgrading your bedding is one of the simplest ways to improve sleep quality. Most folks need a new mattress every 8 to 10 years and new pillows (good ones) every two years or so. Replace old sheets, blankets, and comforters periodically to maximize comfort and adjust to your changing needs as you age. Yes, you'll spend more than pocket change doing this, but consider it an investment in your well-being.

Space – The final frontier – at least right before you fall asleep. This is rarely, if ever, mentioned in the medical literature, but we need adequate space or room for good quality sleep. Over the years I've encountered dozens of couples who kept each other awake tossing and turning in an old double bed. Even a queen size bed is not roomy enough for many couples. Too many pillows or heavy, restrictive bedding can interfere with range of motion during the night. Feeling confined and cramped is not conducive to relaxation or restful sleep. Give yourself and your spouse the space you need. Which brings us to the final bedroom blunder...

Spouse – Brace yourself for a bruised ego, hurt feelings, whining, sulking, and assorted other immature responses. If you share a bed with someone, it's unlikely you're both incredibly sound sleepers. More often than not, one person conks out while the other lies awake frustrated by his or her partner's restless sleep, thrashing, snoring, trips to the bathroom, etc., etc., etc. The solution may well be found in separate beds or dare I say it, separate rooms. This decision to sleep separately does not mean that the relationship is in trouble. In fact, in the long run, this approach may save the relationship. Unfortunately, people tend to be very sensitive and defensive about sleeping arrangements. But love has nothing to do with insomnia, restless legs syndrome, parasomnias, or sleep apnea. If you know perfectly well the other person is keeping you awake, simply try sleeping apart for a week or two. If there is no improvement, you can always return to your original arrangements. Intimacy need not suffer, but if one of you is chronically sleep-deprived intimacy won't last long anyway.

To sum it up, if you like sleeping poorly, be sure your bedroom stays overheated, bright, noisy, cluttered, uncomfortable, and overcrowded. That should do it.

9. Daytime Naps

If you grew up in a culture where taking an afternoon siesta was part of the daily routine, ignore this. Most of us, however, haven't had regular naps since kindergarten. Nearly everyone experiences a mid-afternoon dip in energy and alertness, which is probably why so many cultures have some version of a siesta in the first place. Our post WWII obsession with efficiency and productivity has fostered a societal suppression of this natural tendency to rest. Just try taking an afternoon nap if you work in health care or the business world. I promise you will not be viewed as someone who is sensibly aligned with the rhythms of nature. So if an afternoon nap is natural, why are we discussing it in this section? Timing, the problem is bad timing. Many people with insomnia aggravate the problem by taking too long a nap too late in the day. Have you ever felt poorly and taken a long nap, then awakened only to feel even worse? I certainly have, especially after having worked all night. An afternoon nap under those conditions can leave me feeling like something that should be embalmed! Feeling worse after a nap can be due to drifting into deep Stage 4 sleep and waking abruptly.[1] Napping too long or late in the day can also interfere with normal sleep patterns at night. Moderation and common sense to the rescue. If you know daytime naps make you feel worse, don't take them. Otherwise, limit naps to 30 minutes and don't nap past 3:00pm (unless you need to be awake late at night). Here's another idea – try a 30-minute period of rest and relaxation in the afternoon without sleeping. More on that in Chapter Eight.

10. Pill Popping

We live in a culture where many people really do believe "if you have a problem, there must be a pill for it." Many people take pills to wake up, calm down, stay alert, unwind, lose weight, stop sneezing, and stop aching. In fact, there are folks who would happily pop pills to start or stop almost any bodily function you can think of. Appropriate use of medication has saved countless lives and alleviated tremendous suffering. But even the best drugs can be misused, overused, or abused. And sometimes perfectly appropriate use of medications can result in unrecognized side effects, including disruption of normal sleep architecture. This happens to be the subject in Chapter Seven. Isn't that convenient?

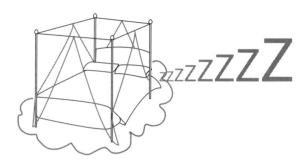

Recommended Reading

1. Perlis ML, Smith MT, Pigeon WR. Etiology and pathophysiology of insomnia. In: Krugger MH, Roth T, Dement WC, eds. *Principles and Practice of Sleep Medicine*. 4th ed. Philadelphia, PA: Elsevier/Saunders,2005: 714-725.

2. Spira AP, Jasdeep SA, Sheikh JI. Link between anxiety and insomnia in the older person. *Clinical Geriatrics*. 2006;14: 17-22.

3. Silber MH. Chronic Insomnia. NEJM.2005;353: 8.803-810.

4. Kamel NS, Gammack JK. Insomnia in the elderly: Cause, Approach and Treatment. *Am J Med*. 2006;119: 463-469.

5. Schenck CH, Mahowald MW, Sack RL. Assessment and management of insomnia. *JAMA* 2003;289: 2475-2479.

6. Ohayon MM, Roth T. What are the contributing factors for insomnia in the general population? *J Psychosom Res*.2001;51: 745-755.

References

1. Buysee DJ, Browman KE, Monk TH, et al. Napping and 24-hour sleep/wake patterns in healthy elderly and young adults. *J Am Ger Soc*. 1992;40(8): 779-786.

Chapter **7**

Medications That May Disrupt Sleep

"When we are unable to find tranquility within ourselves, it is useless to seek it elsewhere."

–Francois de La Rochefoucauld
French author & moralist
(1613 - 1680)

Anyone involved in health care today has encountered patients on 22, 23, or 24 prescription drugs. Most of these drugs have never been studied in combination with one another and, frankly, we have no idea how most of them affect sleep architecture. We do, however, know that certain classes of drugs can wreak havoc with sleep. Caffeine, nicotine, and alcohol can be big offenders, as we discussed in Chapter Six. These substances tend to interfere with continuity of sleep. Some medications disrupt sleep by stimulating the central nervous system (CNS). Others actually exacerbate primary sleep disorders. And some medications cause so much daytime sedation that nighttime sleep is compromised. Millions of people really do believe there's a pill for every problem. As we're about to see, that mindset can lead to some very frustrating, long nights.

Antihistamines

Many people take medications like diphenhydramine to get a better night's sleep. Over-the-counter preparations like Benadryl (diphenhydramine) or Tylenol PM (acetaminophen and diphenhydramine) fall into this category. While their sedating effects may facilitate falling asleep, their anticholinergic side effects can be significant, especially in older individuals. The anticholinergic side effects include daytime drowsiness, dry eyes, dry mouth, constipation, urinary retention, confusion, tachycardia, and ataxia (problems with balance and coordination). Anticholinergic drugs work against acetylcholine. Acetylcholine is the single most important neurotransmitter for memory. It's also the neurotransmitter that is most deficient in Alzheimer's disease.

> Acetylcholine is the single most important neurotransmitter for memory.

Taking any drug that works against acetylcholine is not a great idea for those of us over the age of 50. The half-life of these drugs is not static as we age. They tend to linger in the body longer as we get older. Best to avoid regular use of older sedating antihistamines if you need to stay sharp in the daytime. Besides, there are no specific data showing that antihistamines actually help insomnia or improve sleep quality.[1] If you absolutely must take an antihistamine for allergies or hay fever, take one of the newer, less sedating medications, like, Claritin (loratadine).

Sympathomimetic Amines

This class of drugs includes medications for asthma and the decongestants. Bronchodilators such as terbutaline, albuterol, salmeterol, metaproterenol, and theophylline have been used for years in patients with asthma or chronic obstructive pulmonary disease (COPD). Also known as beta-agonists, these drugs interfere with sleep by stimulating the central nervous system. Well-recognized side effects include a restless, jittery feeling, tremulousness, and tachycardia. Generally speaking, beta-agonist inhalers are better tolerated and usually do not adversely affect sleep.[2] In managing chronic lung patients, balancing pulmonary function with sleep quality requires careful adjustment of medication regimens.

Nasal decongestants in cold and flu preparations can also stimulate the central nervous system and disrupt sleep. Years ago, phenylpropanolamine was a common culprit, but it is no longer an over-the-counter (OTC) product. Pseudoephedrine has become a "behind the counter" component of cold and flu products because of concerns about its abuse in "crystal-meth-rings." Phenylephrine is being used more often in cough and cold medications, but it is considered less effective by many people and has significant side effects, including irritability, arrhythmias, dizziness, headache, drowsiness, and even seizures. Every drug has its downside, so it's important to monitor your own response to common OTC products.

Beta-blockers are capable of suppressing melatonin production.

Antihypertensive Medications

A number of older blood pressure drugs can produce daytime somnolence, thereby interfering with sleep at night. Clonidine, methyldopa, and reserpine would be included in this category. A more commonly used class of antihypertensives, the beta-blockers, can also disrupt sleep through several mechanisms. Beta-blockers (pindolol,

Metoprolol [lopressor], Propranolol [inderal]) are capable of suppressing melatonin production.[3] In healthy volunteers, beta-blockers increased the likelihood of remembered dreams, increased the perceived number of awakenings, and disrupted continuity of sleep after one week.[4,5] Interestingly, Atenolol (tenormin) did not affect sleep in any significant fashion. Low dose beta-blockers have been used for many years in the treatment of panic attacks, anxiety disorders and post traumatic stress disorder. In these sorts of clinical situations, appropriate use of beta-blockers may blunt the physical manifestation of anxiety and actually facilitate sleep.

Hormones

Several commonly prescribed hormones can interfere with sleep. Some women experience sleep disruption while taking oral contraceptives or progesterone, and there seems to be considerable individual variation here. Initiation of treatment with thyroid replacement (i.e., Synthroid [levothyroxine sodium]) or even mild overreplacement when attempting to fine-tune dosing can result in insomnia. Often this problem is accompanied by other symptoms such as tachycardia, jitteriness, increased appetite, or weight loss.

The most frequent and troublesome sleep problems occur during treatment with glucocorticoids (prednisone, dexamethasone). Glucocorticoids, or steroids, are known to decrease total sleep time and reduce sleep efficiency (time asleep relative to time spent in bed).[6] Perhaps you have had the experience of taking a Medrol Dose-Pak (methylprednisolone) for poison ivy or some other short-term condition and felt "too wired" to sleep. Most of us can tolerate this for a week or so, and it's not a big deal. But in many cases, steroids are prescribed for much more serious conditions like asthma, COPD, lupus, multiple sclerosis (MS), vasculitis, and numerous others. In situations like these, abrupt discontinuation of steroids is simply not an option. Restoring sleep can be challenging in these settings and usually requires comprehensive therapy, including careful attention to sleep hygiene or habits, cognitive behavioral therapy, and, in many cases, specific use of prescription sleep medications.

Neurologic Drugs

This is a fairly large category, and includes anti-seizure medications like Dilantin (phenytoin), Lamictal (lamotrigine), and Topamax (topiramate). In recent years, Topamax (topiramate) has also been used in the treatment of chronic pain and to reduce the frequency of migraine headaches. A number of antipsychotic medications is capable of exacerbating insomnia (Risperdal [risperidone], Haldol [haloperidol], Abilify [aripiprazole]). Others may increase daytime drowsiness, thereby interfering with sleep at night (i.e., Lithium, Mellaril [thioridazine], Seroquel [quetiapine], and Zyprexa [olanzapine]). It's important to note that these drugs can also exacerbate restless legs syndrome and periodic limbic movement disorder.

Medications for Parkinson's disease are frequent contributors to insomnia.

Several anticonvulsant drugs seem to have variable effects on sleep, which can lead to a clinical dilemma. Patients with epilepsy generally experience a sleep-enhancing effect from drugs such as Dilantin (phenytoin), valproic acid, or Tegretol (carbamazepine). In seizure patients, these drugs have been shown to shorten sleep latency (speed sleep onset) and increase the time spent in deep sleep.[7,8] Tegretol (carbamazepine) may also fragment rapid eye movement (REM) sleep in patients with temporal lobe epilepsy for at least the first month of therapy.[9] Neurontin or gabapentin is used in seizure patients and also as adjunctive therapy in chronic pain patients. It may cause daytime somnolence and fatigue and yet, some patients feel they sleep better, possibly as a result of improved pain control.

Medications for Parkinson's disease are frequent contributors to insomnia. They can also cause daytime somnolence, hallucinations, and disturbing dreams. Upsetting dreams or night terrors are extremely disruptive and exhausting for the patient, family members, caregivers, or other nearby patients in the hospital or nursing home. Parkinson's medications are notoriously difficult to fine-tune, and constant adjustment may be necessary. Drugs in this category include various forms of Sinemet (carbidopa-levodopa), Mirapex (pramipexole), Parlodel (bromocriptine), and Requip (ropinirole).

Another important class of neurologic medications is the stimulants used in the management of attention-deficit/hyperactivity disorder (ADHD) and narcolepsy. Examples include Adderall (amphetamine salt combo), Concerta (methylphenidate), Daytrana patch (methylphenidate), Dexedrine (dextroamphetamine), Focalin (exmethylphenidate), and Ritalin (methylphenidate).

Provigil (modafinil) is used in narcolepsy to improve wakefulness and in severe obstructive sleep apnea. It may also be used to maintain wakefulness in people with shift work sleep disorder. Strattera (atomoxetine) is a newer non-stimulant drug for adult and pediatric ADHD. It is a selective norepinephrine reuptake inhibitor (SNRI) that may cause either daytime somnolence or insomnia.

Finally, any of the acetylcholinesterase inhibitors for Alzheimer's disease can interfere with sleep. They often cause daytime sleepiness but are certainly capable of aggravating

insomnia. These medications include Aricept (donepezil), Exelon (rivastigmine), and Razadyne (galantamine). Namenda (memantine) is an N-methyl-D-aspartate receptor antagonist. Translation in normal-person English: it works on glutamate levels in the brain. Consequently, Namenda (memantine) can worsen daytime somnolence and induce hallucinations in some people. Obviously, where medications are concerned, we must always weigh the potential benefits against potential side effects. And that is invariably a patient-by-patient judgment call.

Any of the acetylcholinesterase inhibitors for Alzheimer's disease can interfere with sleep.

Antidepressants

This is another large category of drugs with varied effects on sleep. The tricyclic antidepressants (i.e, Elavil [amitriptyline], Pamelor [nortriptyline], Norpramin [desipramine]) generally improve sleep latency and sleep continuity in depressed patients with insomnia. In fact, improvement in insomnia is one of the earliest benefits when a depressed patient begins therapy with a tricyclic antidepressant (TCA).[10] Sleep studies in depressed patients taking TCAs reveal increased total sleep time and better slow-wave sleep.[11] Taking one of the TCAs if you're depressed and having trouble sleeping may be helpful, but many doctors prescribe these medications as primary sleeping pills. That is not a good idea. Drugs in the tricyclic class have significant anticholinergic side effects, just as antihistamines do – dry eyes, dry mouth, constipation, urinary retention, confusion, tachycardia, and ataxia. Most geriatricians would advise against giving these medications to people over age 60.

In a class by itself, literally, is Desyrel (trazodone), an older nontricyclic antidepressant. This drug also has sedating properties and seems to improve sleep in depressed patients with insomnia. However, after initial improvement in insomnia, trazodone was shown to be no better than placebo after two weeks in non-depressed people with insomnia.[12] In my experience, very few people can take trazodone and be sharp as a tack at 6:00 am. Again, this is not a good choice for older individuals, non-depressed people, or folks who actually need to function at a high level.

The most frequently prescribed antidepressants over the past 20 years are the selective serotonin reuptake inhibitors (SSRIs). Drugs in this class include Prozac (fluoxetine), Paxil (paroxetine), Zoloft (sertraline), Celexa (citalopram), and Lexapro (escitalopram). These drugs have been shown to reduce sleep efficiency, delay sleep onset, and increase the number of nighttime awakenings.[13]

Prozac (fluoxetine), the first SSRI to be approved in 1987, is associated with a 10% incidence of treatment-induced insomnia.[14] In sleep studies, Prozac (fluoxetine) has been shown to disrupt sleep continuity in depressed adults.[15] Paxil (paroxetine) has been demonstrated to prolong sleep latency (time it takes to fall asleep) and disturb sleep architecture in non-depressed adults with insomnia.[16]

Another important class of antidepressant medications is described as serotonin-norepinephrine reuptake inhibitors (SNRIs). Drugs in this class include Effexor (venlafaxine) and

Cymbalta (duloxetine). These drugs have similar effects on sleep when compared to the SSRIs. They can increase daytime somnolence and exacerbate insomnia in some people. Once again, before tossing drugs at patients we need to consider carefully the potential benefits as well as the potential side effects.

Analgesics

Pain medications often have variable effects on sleep. Over-the-counter headache remedies containing caffeine can certainly delay sleep onset. Opiates (i.e., codeine, hydrocodone, oxycodone, morphine) often cause daytime somnolence, which can interfere with nighttime sleep. However, if pain, especially severe pain, has been keeping a patient awake at night, adequate pain relief may be the ticket for a good night's sleep. Ultram (tramadol) is a centrally-acting analgesic with unique properties. Over the years, I have encountered patients who experience good pain relief, but they complained of feeling sleepy yet unable to fall asleep when they took Ultram (tramadol) in the evening. Similarly, the triptan drugs for migraines (i.e., Imitrex [sumatriptan],

Zomig [zolmitriptan], Relpax [eletriptan]) may increase daytime sleepiness with variable results at night. The best bet here is to be observant and engage in a little common sense.

Antineoplastic Agents

Anyone coping with cancer has multiple reasons to struggle with sleep – pain, nausea, daytime fatigue, anxiety, and depression, just to name a few. However, a number of chemotherapeutic drugs can aggravate insomnia:

Chemotherapeutic Drugs		
Brand Name	Generic Name	Used For:
Provera, (many brands)	Medroxyprogesterone	Endometriosis, multiple conditions
Aromasin	Exemestane	Advanced breast cancer
Femara	Letrozole	Breast cancer
Gleevec	Imatinib	Prostate or breast cancer
Lupron	Leuprolide	Anemia caused by uterine tumors
Adriamycin	Daunorubicin	Various malignancies
Intron A, PEG-Intron	Interferon alpha	Hepatitis C

Patients receiving any of these drugs (and often surgery and radiation therapy) may require prescription sleep medications for several weeks or months at a time.

Miscellaneous Medications

Every list in medicine has a "miscellaneous" category – it's a rule! Two significant classes of drugs are often overlooked as sleep disrupters. Diuretics, used in the treatment of hypertension and congestive heart failure, can precipitate multiple nocturnal trips to the bathroom, especially if they are taken after mid-day. Diuretics are best taken first thing in the morning.

The other contender is overly aggressive use of oral hypoglycemic agents. If the patient's blood sugar drops too low at night, a rebound phenomenon can occur that involves increased adrenaline levels. This can leave a very fatigued and uncomfortable patient wide-awake in the middle of the night. Careful and frequent blood glucose monitoring, combined with awareness of a potential problem, is the best way to address this concern.

References

1. Ancoli-Israel S. Sleep problems in older adults: putting myths to bed. *Geriatrics.* 1997; 52: 20-30.

2. McCall WV. *A practical guide to insomnia.* McGraw-Hill, Minneapolis. 20004; 24-25.

3. Barczi SR. Medical Illness, Medications and Sleep in Older Adults; in Sleep Disorders, Supplement to Clinical Geriatrics. December 2005; 12.

4. Betts TA, Alford C. Beta blockers and sleep: a controlled trial. *Eur J Clin Pharmacol.* 1985; 28 (Suppl): 65-68.

5. Kortis JB, Rosen RC. Central nervous system effects of beta adrenergic blocking drugs: the role of ancillary properties. *Circulation.* 1987; 75 (1): 204-212.

6. Fehm HL, Benkowitsch R, Fehm-Wolfsdorf G, et al. Influences of corticosteroids, dexamethasone and hydrocortisone on sleep in humans. *Neuropsychobiology.* 1986;16(4):198-204.

7. Harding GF, Alford CH, Powell TE. The effect of sodium valproate on sleep, reaction times, and visual evoked potential in normal subjects. *Epilepsia.* 1985; 26 (6): 597-601.

8. Roder-Wanner UU, Noachtar S, Wolf P. Response of polygraphic sleep to phenytoin treatment for epilepsy. A longitudinal study of immediate, short and long term effects. *Acta Neurol Scand.* 1987; 76 (3):157-167.

9. Gigli, GL, Placidi F, Diomedi M, et al. Nocturnal sleep and daytime somnolence in untreated patients with temporal lobe epilepsy: changes after treatment with controlled-release carbamazepine. *Epilepsia.* 1997;38(6):696-701.

10. Di Marcio A, Weissman MM, Prusoff BA, et al. Differential symptom reduction by drugs and psychotherapy in acute depression. *Arch Gen Psychiatry.* 1979;6(30):1450-1456.

11. Kupfer DJ. The sleep EEG in diagnosis and treatment of depression. Depression: basic mechanisms, diagnosis, and treatment. New York, NY; Guilford Press, 1986:102-125.

12. Walsh JK, Erman M, Erwin GW, et al. Subjective hypnotic efficacy of trazodone and zolpidem in DSM-III-R primary insomnia. Human *Psychopharmacol Clin Exper.* 1998; 13: 5191-5198.

13. Barczi SR. Medical illness, medications and sleep in older adults. Supplement to Clinical Geriatrics. Dec. 2005; 10-12.

14. Beasley CM Jr, Nilsson BE, Koke SC, et al. Efficacy, adverse events and treatment discontinuations in fluoxetine clinical studies of major depression: a meta-analysis of the 20 mg/day dose. *J Clin Psychiatry.* 2000; 61 (10): 722-728.

15. Gillin JC, Rapaport M, Erman MK, et al. A comparison of nefazodone and fluoxetine on mood and on objective, subjective, and clinician-rated measures of sleep in depressed patients: a double-blind, 8 week clinical trial. *J Clin Psychiatry.* 1997;58(5):185-192.

16. Nowell PD, Reynolds CF 3rd, Buysse DJ, et al. Paroxetine in the treatment of primary insomnia: preliminary clinical and electroencephalogram sleep data. *J Clin Psychiatry.* 1999;60(2): 89-95.

Chapter **8**

Healthy Sleep Habits

"Three enemies of personal peace: regrets over yesterday's mistakes, anxiety over tomorrow's problems, and ingratitude for today's blessings."

—William A. Ward
Inspirational Writer
(1921 - 1994)

Once the major sleep-stealing culprits have been identified, custom-tailored treatment can begin. Television commercials would have us believe that treatment of choice involves prescription drugs, and the more expensive, the better. Medications can be immensely helpful in specific situations, but non-drug measures should almost always be attempted first. If insomnia is secondary to medical illness or pain, the illness or pain requires better management. If medications are interfering with sleep, adjusting their dose or timing may improve sleep quality. And, since anxiety almost always plays a role in perpetuating insomnia, setting reasonable expectations and cultivating a healthy approach to relaxation can help immensely.

Behavioral therapies include interventions such as relaxation exercises, sleep restriction, stimulus control, and cognitive therapy. The common goal here is to quiet autonomic nervous system arousal and correct dysfunctional beliefs that exacerbate insomnia.[1]

Consider the main principles of each:

Relaxation Techniques

Some people respond well to the calming effect of progressive muscle relaxation, breathing exercises, biofeedback, yoga, and meditation. With the exception of biofeedback, all of these practices can be learned using audio tapes, CDs, or DVDs. Deliberate efforts to unwind and decompress can make falling asleep easier. However, it's often better to practice these techniques during the day. The focused, goal-directed effort of learning a new skill may work against the passive nature of falling asleep.[2] Practicing any of these techniques over time reduces the feeling of having to "work at it." A major bonus effect of relaxation exercises such as yoga and meditation is a potential reduction in heart rate and blood pressure.

Stimulus-Control Therapy

This approach limits the use of the bedroom to sleeping and sexual activity to re-establish an association between bed and sleep. Appropriate patients would be those with irregular sleep-wake habits and those who frequently use their bedroom for everything but sleep – working, reading, studying, eating, surfing the net, and watching television. This would probably include half of America. Stimulus-control therapy is based on the assumption that insomnia is a maladaptive response that needs to be corrected.[3] Patients are instructed not to go to bed until they are really sleepy. They've also been told to get up and go to another room if they can't fall asleep within 10 minutes. Staying in bed while alert or anxious about not sleeping reinforces the association between bed and wakefulness. This is a great way to perpetuate insomnia. Any relatively quiet activity may be pursued while waiting for sleepiness to develop. Patients are counseled to wake up at their usual time in the morning and avoid daytime naps.

Sleep-Restriction Therapy

This strategy also attempts to correct or break the unhealthy association of the bed with wakefulness. Patients are advised to limit their time in bed to their estimated total sleep time, as long as that does not drop below 4.5 hours. Morning wake-up time remains the same. Once the patients believe they are asleep 90% of the time they're in bed, over a five-day period, they may go to bed a bit earlier. Gradually, the amount of time in bed can be increased. This approach has been used since the mid-1980s with some success.[4]

Cognitive Behavioral Therapy

The goal of cognitive behavioral therapy (CBT) is to challenge dysfunctional beliefs and expectations about sleep and address the resultant anxiety and catastrophic thinking. It is generally regarded as the treatment of choice for chronic, primary insomnia. CBT often incorporates basic principles of good sleep hygiene as well as stimulus control and sleep restriction. It is certainly more time-consuming than taking a pill, since several 30 to 60 minute sessions with a trained therapist are usually required. Unfortunately, most physicians don't have this sort of time or training, and insurance rarely pays for the therapy. This problem needs to be addressed since CBT can improve sleep latency, sleep maintenance, sleep quality, and total sleep time.[5] Interestingly, a study published in 2006 demonstrated that therapy based on

CBT was superior to zoplicone (a drug similar to Lunesta [eszopiclone]) in both short- and long-term treatment of insomnia.[6] This drug is available in Norway, but not in the United States. CBT may be especially helpful for sleep onset insomnia with improvement in sleep latency and sleep efficiency, maintained at 12-month follow-up.[7] The most effective sleeping pill on the planet doesn't help insomnia 12 months later.

> Exercising in the late afternoon or early evening can facilitate sleep.

There's no doubt that cognitive or psychological interventions for primary insomnia are helpful. But trained therapists are scarce in most areas, and cost can be significant. And of course, we have the ever-present issue of time. Speaking as someone who could single-handedly raise insomnia to an Olympic-caliber event, I can't imagine finding the time to pursue multiple CBT sessions. Being overextended is already a major factor for most of us when it comes to insomnia. Fortunately, there are simple, practical tips that can improve sleep time and quality. The straightforward measures below come under the peculiar heading of "sleep hygiene." (I still don't understand what soap and water have to do with this.)

1. Benefit from a regular routine. I know this sounds dull, but most of us sleep better when we wake up and go to bed at the same time every day. Weekends, holidays, and vacations included. If you struggle with insomnia, please try this for several weeks. If, after three weeks of a regular sleep routine, insomnia is still problematic, you can always resume your erratic ways (and pay for a sleep therapist to give you the same advice).

2. Increase exposure to bright light or sunshine as soon as you wake up. Don't amble around in the dark for an hour. This is a simple way to help the suprachiasmatic nucleus do its job and regulate day/night cycles.

3. Spend time outdoors late in the afternoon or early in the evening. Remember, living like one of the "mole people" will not help insomnia. Human sleep cycles are heavily dependent on light levels in nature.

4. __Let your body get as tired as your mind__. This means engaging in the "E" word (or exercise) on a regular basis. Sitting in front of the television or computer screen all evening will not enhance your sleep. Exercising in the late afternoon or early evening can facilitate sleep. The only caution is to avoid major exercise within three hours of bedtime, so that over-stimulation is not a problem.

5. __Develop a relaxing routine before bed__. Consistently sending your brain relaxation signals in the evening invites better quality sleep. A bubble bath, skin care regimens, a little meditation or prayer time, reading something pleasant, setting out clothes and accessories for the next day, are good ways to decompress.

6. __Turn the alarm clock backwards__. Digital clocks with their big, bold luminescent numbers produce enough light to disrupt sleep in light-sensitive people. Everyone who's ever spent a frustrating night watching the alarm clock, raise your hand! Okay, that was about all of us. Turn the alarm clock away from you – it will still ring in the morning.

7. **Avoid the "nap trap."** Resist the temptation to nap even after a sleepless night. If you absolutely must lie down, do it before 3:00 pm, and don't nap longer than 30 minutes. Avoiding naps helps preserve incentive to sleep at night.

8. **Keep your bedroom cool & your feet warm.** No kidding. The optimum temperature for sleep is somewhere between 65 F° and 67 F°. That's my idea of chilly, but it actually enhances melatonin production. Curiously, having a cool face but warm hands and feet induces sleep more quickly.[8] Socks are not very sexy, but then neither are ice-cold feet.

9. **Take a warm bath 30 minutes before bedtime.** The act of relaxing in a warm bath makes sense after a hectic day, but the rationale for the advice extends beyond relaxation. Soaking in a warm bath causes mild overheating

and vasodilation. Stepping out of the tub and drying off is accompanied by a slight chilling effect. The temperature differential (being very warm and then cooling off) stimulates the pineal gland to produce more melatonin. Isn't it great when pleasant activities enhance normal physiologic function? This tip really does qualify as "sleep hygiene!"

10. Don't go to bed unless you're actually sleepy. What a concept! This is a key component of stimulus control therapy. Engaging in quiet activities for an hour or so before bedtime helps unmask sleepiness (i.e., reading, knitting, crocheting, and journaling).

11. Get a grip on your worries. Free-floating anxiety does not enhance sleep architecture. Write down a list of your concerns/worries/problems/issues in the evening and put it aside. Do the same with a "to-do list" for the next day. Writing things down is curiously comforting. It also does wonders for daytime efficiency.

201 The Healing Power of Sleep

12. <u>Have a light bedtime snack</u>. The operative word here is "light." Going to bed 10 minutes after eating half a pizza is a great way to wake up with heartburn. Going to bed with an empty stomach is a great way to wake up at 2:00 am with hunger pangs. Light snacks that are gastrointestinal-friendly include a couple of graham crackers and four ounces of milk, a custard cup of whole grain cereal (that's custard cup, not mixing bowl), a half-cup of pudding or yogurt, a piece of toast. Avoid anything that's heavy, greasy, spicy, or difficult to digest.

13. <u>Ease up on evening liquids</u>. We seem to have developed a national obsession with drinking lots of fluids. People practically have bottles of water surgically implanted into the palms of their hands. But consuming liquids after 8:00 pm is a wonderful way to end up with nocturia. Multiple trips to the bathroom at night can lead to a miserable morning.

14. <u>Keep your bedroom dark and quiet</u>. We already addressed the alarm clock issue. But wait – there's more. A list of luminescent or digital contraptions can interfere with sleep by stimulating the reticular activating system of the brain: lights on a smoke detector, clocks, radio/CD players, security lights, night lights, air purifiers, etc. Perhaps a street light or even the moon disrupts your sleep some nights. Consider a drapery clip, light-blocking blinds, or even the black drapes used in Alaska to block out "midnight sun." Noise often wreaks havoc with sleep as well. Turn the phone's ringer off; keep the television or radio volume low in the evening; keep office equipment with its assorted beeps, clicks, and humming out of your bedroom. Keep earplugs readily accessible when all else fails.

15. <u>Try to avoid work within two hours of bedtime</u>. Wait – is someone playing, "The Impossible Dream" in the background? The days of leaving work behind at the end of the day are over. The information highway has tunneled right into our bedrooms. Enough. The last two hours of the day should belong to you – not your boss. Plan something pleasant, quiet, romantic, relaxing, soothing, creative, or contemplative before bedtime. No apologies necessary.

16. **Invest in quality bedding.** We've already discussed this one. Most folks need a new mattress every 10 years or so. Pillows don't last that long. Before you go to bed tonight, fold your pillow in half. Release it. If it stays folded, it's broken! Don't try to sleep on a flat old pancake pillow. Find the right blend of comfort and support, and don't be cheap! Invest in new pillows about every two years. One more tip – wash your pillowcases every other day, especially if hay fever, allergies, sinus problems, or cold and flu bugs abound.

17. **Serenade yourself to sleep.** Music specifically composed to induce sleep is readily available on CD's. In fact, Crowne Plaza Hotels provide a CD with progressive relaxation exercises and tranquil music. Speaking as a frequent traveler with hard-core insomnia, their CD is remarkably helpful. Similar products are available through sleep medicine clinics, catalogs, and professional organizations. Best to be certain that the CD shuts off after 30 minutes or so. Sleep can be disturbed by even soft music, especially in light sleepers and insomnia patients.

18. Don't "try" to sleep. Hard-driving, ambitious, go-getter, type-A people with overactive minds (I know someone just like that) tend to think they can do almost anything if they just try hard enough. And, they're right – about nearly every endeavor except sleep. Sleep cannot be forced, chosen, or decided upon. Sleep comes as a result of letting go of wakefulness. No wonder so many of us struggle!

19. Don't drink caffeine after mid-afternoon & avoid alcohol after dinner. The why's and wherefore's are in Chapter Six.

20. Don't smoke. Ever.

21. Just say "no" to your cell phone (or any other communication device) within two hours of bedtime. This may elicit withdrawal symptoms in susceptible individuals. There was a time when people had manners and didn't pester other people after 8:00 pm or 9:00 pm. Today, most folks are clueless on this score. The mere act of responding to a ringing phone alerts the sympathetic nervous system. Bad idea right before bed. Tell your friends, family, and colleagues to leave you alone in the evening. Maybe they'll sleep better, too. (As I write this, researchers at the University of Zurich are studying the effects of electromagnetic waves from cell phones on brain wave patterns during sleep!)

22. <u>Abandon the big screen TV</u>. Stop groaning. A massive wide screen television can provide far too much stimulation to the reticular activating system, especially late at night when we're supposed to be settling down. Years ago television screens were much smaller and dimmer. Insomnia was not a national epidemic. If you struggle with insomnia, try going back to the small television (without surround sound), tone down the brightness and turn down the volume. If it doesn't help after a couple of weeks you can always go back to assaulting your senses. (If sitting in front of a 72" screen with surround sound doesn't disturb your sleep, you're probably a man.)

23. <u>Use light to your advantage</u>. When you have to be alert, active, and productive, keep light levels high. This is helpful if you work nights or if you tend to get sleepy too early in the evening. When it's dark at 5:00 pm, I can feel sleepy by 6:30 pm. But that's a great way to be wide-awake at midnight or develop advanced sleep-phase syndrome. Keep the lights bright and stay active until 8:00 pm to 8:30 pm in the evening, then go throughout the house and gradually dim the lights. Dim the lights in the kitchen, the family room, the living room, and your bedroom. Every 30 minutes or so, dim them a bit more until you're ready for bed and the house is almost dark. This is a strategy I dreamed up to deal with my own insomnia. It mimics the gradual light level changes in nature. There's nothing natural about having every electric light or gadget in the house on full strength one minute and off the next. One more thing. If you have to get up at night to use the bathroom, don't flip on the light. It can send the wrong message to the suprachiasmatic nucleus and pineal gland. Keep a night light in the bathroom (or kitchen) and spare yourself an excessively rude awakening.

> If you have to get up at night, don't flip on the light.

24. <u>Pretend you're royalty & sleep alone.</u> For hundreds of years, members of aristocracy maintained separate bedrooms because they could afford to. Peasants had no choice but to huddle together in the same tiny bed. If your spouse, partner, or significant other is destroying your sleep because of snoring, restless legs syndrome, periodic limb movement disorder, nightmares, nocturia, or assorted other disorders, encourage them to get help and go to the guestroom. It's astonishing how many people are reluctant even to have this discussion. They're afraid their spouse will get upset and start sulking. (I've had this discussion with hundreds of patients over the past 30 years). It doesn't have to be a permanent arrangement, although many couples eventually realize they both sleep better separately. Sleeping in separate rooms makes a lot of sense if one person is sick with a cold or flu, GI problems, chronic pain, or other challenges. The person who is ill feels less inhibited about tossing and turning or getting up and down during the night. The decision to try separate beds or separate rooms is not a reflection on the relationship or level of love. It's a matter of common sense and maturity. Sometimes getting a good night's sleep is a question of growing up.

25. <u>Put puppy & kitty in their proper place</u> – in another room. Yes, I'm giving this sermon again. There are probably vast numbers of people who would rather sleep without their spouse than forego the presence of their pet. However, this issue requires brutal honesty. If you sleep like a log with your pet on the bed, don't change. But if noise and motion from Fluffy disrupts your sleep throughout the night, something needs to change. Even a quiet pet may disrupt sleep

> When you have to be alert, active and productive, keep light levels high.

by triggering nasal congestion and allergies. People tend to be very stubborn about this issue, to the point of being irrational. Consult your veterinarian about ways to break bad sleep habits. Your furry friend needs you to be healthy, and that requires decent sleep.

26. <u>**Address emotional & spiritual issues.**</u> This is clearly a life-long endeavor and will not eliminate the occasional sleepless night. But many of us are seriously overextended and over stimulated and could benefit from more quiet reflection, meditation, prayer, or contemplative time. Emerson had a great perspective on this, "Prayer is the contemplation of the facts of life from the highest point of view." All of us go through times of stress, worry, conflict, grief, loss, frustration, and disappointment. Avoiding the real issue never really solves it. Develop a confidante, go for counseling, read an uplifting book, listen to inspiring talks, audio tapes, CD's. Go for a long walk. Spend time in a dark, quiet church. Watch the sunset, the moonrise, and listen to your heart.

There's a time and place for pills as we'll see in the next chapter, but medical wisdom can still be summed up in the words of Moliere back in 1665, "The mind has great influence over the body, and maladies often have their origin there."

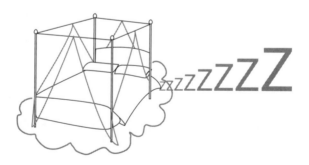

References

1. Kamel NS, Gammack JK. Insomnia in the elderly: cause, approach and treatment. *Am J of Med.* 2006;119: 463-469.

2. Neubauer DN. Treatment of insomnia: What works – what doesn't. *Consultant.* 2005 (suppl) 45;13: 514-523.

3. Silber MH. Chronic insomnia. *N Eng J Med.* 2005;353: 803-810.

4. Sateia MJ, Nowell PD. Insomnia. *Lancet.* 2004;364: 1959-1973.

5. Silvertsen B, Omvik S, Pallesen S, et al. Cognitive Behavioral therapy vs Zopiclone for treatment of chronic primary insomnia in older adults. *JAMA.* 2006;295:2851-2858.

6. Sivertsen B, Omvik S, Pallesen S, et al. Cognitive behavioral therapy vs zopiclone for treatment of chronic primary insomnia in older adults. *JAMA.* 2006;295:2851-2858.

7. Jacobs GD, Pace-Schott EF, Stickgold R, et al. Cognitive behavior therapy for insomnia: a randomized controlled trial and direct comparison. *Arch Intern Med.* 2004;164:1888-1896.

8. Mayo Clinic Women's HealthSource. Special Report. Nov. 2003.

Chapter 9

Medications for Sleep: The Good, the Bad, and the Highly Questionable

"Extreme remedies are very appropriate for extreme diseases."

—Hippocrates (400 B.C.)

"Most men die of their remedies, not of their diseases."

—Molieré (1673)

What a difference 2,000 years make! The truth is both sentiments are accurate. And, we see evidence of that in every hospital across the country every day of the week. Insomnia, of course, is not an extreme disease, but it can certainly make your life miserable. Chronic insomnia can aggravate heart disease, endocrine disorders, musculoskeletal problems, immune dysfunction, neurologic illness, and psychiatric disorders. Observing the principles of good sleep habits we've discussed is key. And, of course, sleep disorders or other medical illnesses must be properly addressed. But that still leaves millions of people who simply need something to help them sleep. So let's consider the options.

Over-the-Counter Options

Let me cut to the chase. They're not great. We're talking about antihistamines here, the main player being diphenhydramine. Over-the-counter medications containing diphenhydramine include Benadryl, Sominex, Nytol, and Tylenol PM. Some preparations toss in a little Tylenol or acetaminophen for aches and pains. That's nice. Here's the problem: diphenhydramine is a postsynaptic histamine-receptor antagonist. Well, doesn't that say it all? Not really. It's also a post-synaptic muscarinic receptor antagonist, which means it causes anticholinergic side effects.[1]

By now we can all recite them together:

1. Dry eyes.

2. Dry mouth.

3. Constipation.

4. Urinary retention.

5. Confusion.

6. Tachycardia.

7. Ataxia.

The number one side effect, however, is drowsiness, which is why so many people take these medications in the first place. Diphenhydramine is easily absorbed and widely distributed through the central nervous system. In young adults, it has an elimination half-life of seven to eight hours. Half-life is the time needed for 50 percent of a given drug to clear the body. But in the elderly its half-life is greatly prolonged and can exceed 100 hours. Can you say cumulative effect? If someone is already taking another medication with anticholinergic activity, say an antidepressant like Elavil (amitriptyline), we've got trouble. Although antihistamines may improve sleep subjectively, their long half-life, numerous side effects, and potential for interactions with other drugs metabolized by the CYP2D6 enzyme pathway in the liver make these drugs a poor choice for most people. If you need to wake up quickly and be sharp first thing in the morning, these drugs are not for you. If you're over age 60, don't even think about it! Remember – these drugs work against acetylcholine. Acetylcholine is the single most important neurotransmitter for memory. It's the most deficient neurotransmitter in Alzheimer's disease. Most of the drugs we use to slow down the ravages of Alzheimer's disease work by protecting acetylcholine (Aricept [donepezil], Razadyne [rivastigmine], Exelon [galantamine]). So why would anyone with a three-digit IQ willingly put something in her body that works against acetylcholine? That is so dumb it's frightening!

Antidepressants

Sedating antidepressants have been prescribed for chronic insomnia with increasing frequency over the past 15 to 20 years.[2] Unfortunately, there are very few well-designed studies to support this practice. Many physicians still mistakenly believe that most patients with insomnia are depressed. While depressed people with insomnia may sleep better with certain antidepressants,[3,4] it's really not good medical practice to toss antidepressants at people who are not clinically depressed. Yet it's done every day of the week. And here's why:

1.   Antidepressants are not considered addictive, despite the fact that abruptly stopping them can cause a withdrawal or discontinuation syndrome.

2.   Generic antidepressants are cheaper than most specifically developed meds for sleep.

Let's tackle one antidepressant at a time. Elavil (amitriptyline) is a tricyclic antidepressant with sedating properties related to its anticholinergic effects (dry eyes, dry mouth, constipation, urinary retention, confusion, tachycardia, and ataxia). In doses ranging from 10 to 50 mg, Elavil is frequently prescribed for sleep. Higher doses are used to treat depression. There is no doubt that hundreds of thousands of people with fibromyalgia have been given this drug. Not generally a good choice! Elavil can also cause postural hypotension, which can be disastrous in older patients. Another very common side effect is weight gain! Using this drug as a sleeping pill in most patients is simply inappropriate. It is, however, cheap. If, for some reason, a tricyclic antidepressant is needed, a secondary amine such as Pamelor or nortriptyline would be a better choice, since it has less prominent anticholinergic side effects.

> It's really not good medical practice to toss antidepressants at people who are not clinically depressed.

Another antidepressant that is often prescribed for sleep is Desyrel (trazodone). Trazodone is a nontricyclic antidepressant with side effects including drowsiness, fatigue, GI symptoms, hypotension, dizziness, dry mouth, and priapism (prolonged erection). It is often prescribed in doses ranging from 50 to 100 mg. This drug is not a good choice for elderly patients and yet it is widely prescribed for sleep in this age group. Depending on one's metabolism, trazodone has a half-life ranging from 5 to 12 hours. Consequently, it often causes residual daytime sedation.[5] Trust me. You don't want your surgeon taking trazodone. If you actually have to be alert and function well during the day, this is probably not the drug for you.

Doxepin or Sinequan is a tricyclic antidepressant (i.e., anticholinergic side effects, weight gain, sexual dysfunction, hypotension, arrhythmias, drug-drug interactions, reduced seizure threshold, and residual daytime sedation) that is also prescribed off-label for sleep. In one study of 47 patients, low-dose doxepin improved sleep latency and total sleep time better than placebo in nondepressed patients with insomnia. However, they had significant rebound insomnia after doxepin was withdrawn.[6] This drug is not a good choice in people who must function well during the day.

Remeron or mirtazapine is a tetracyclic antidepressant

that has been shown to reduce wake time after sleep onset, enhance sleep efficiency, and increase duration of slow-wave sleep in normal subjects.[7] Unfortunately, data are lacking on the effects of mirtazapine in people with primary insomnia. This drug is sometimes used in geriatric patients with depression to boost appetite. Enough said.

The selective serotonin re-uptake inhibitors (SSRIs) include drugs such as Prozac (fluoxetine), Paxil (paroxetine), Zoloft (sertaline), and Celexa (lexapro). These drugs are frequently prescribed for insomnia – again because of the widespread belief that insomnia is due to depression. The reality, however, is that these drugs do very little to promote sleep. In fact, as we've discussed, the SSRIs can actually interfere with sleep quality.

Benzodiazepines

Long, long ago, in our very own galaxy, doctors dished out long-acting benzodiazepines (tranquilizers) as sleeping pills: Valium (diazepam), Librium (chlordiazepoxide), Doral (quazepam), and lest we forget, Dalmane (flurazepam). Long-acting is an understatement. The active metabolites of these drugs have half-life ranges of 50 to 100 hours or more.[8] That translates into a neurologic nightmare of confusion, memory loss, daytime sedation, motor vehicle accidents, falls, and fractures. We've known for years that falls and their related complications are the leading cause of accidental death in geriatric patients. Falls also play a role in 40% of all nursing home admissions.[9] Benzodiazepine use in the elderly can and frequently does mimic delirium and even dementia.

Before we go on, I should probably stop for a minute and explain how benzodiazepines work. Benzodiazepines bind to GABA (gamma-amino-butyric acid) receptors. GABA is an inhibitory neurotransmitter. I think of it as being the neurotransmitter that "soft pedals" the brain – it keeps too many stimuli from reaching the cerebral cortices. Most anticonvulsant or anti-epileptic drugs also work on GABA receptors. That alone speaks volumes.

There is evidence that benzodiazepines improve sleep by reducing nocturnal awakenings and decreasing sleep latency[10] (the time it takes to fall asleep). Unfortunately, they also tend to suppress rapid eye movement (REM) sleep, which we now know is quite important. Aging does not interfere with benzodiazepine absorption; however, as a consequence of decreased lean body mass, reduced plasma proteins, and increased body fat, we see an increased concentration of unbound drug and prolonged elimination of half-life.[11] Translation in normal person English: these drugs hang around a long time as we get older. In fact, if someone took Dalmane on a nightly basis, the half-life is so long it would never actually be cleared from her body!

Using Xanax or Ativan for sleep is generally regarded as inappropriate today.

Although benzodiazepines are extremely effective in promoting and prolonging sleep initially, with continued use tolerance develops rapidly.[12] Higher and higher doses may become necessary to obtain the original effect. Rebound insomnia can develop with only a week or two of use. And, worst of all, addiction can easily develop into a long-term recalcitrant problem.

The intermediate-acting benzodiazepines have a half-life in the 6- to 24-hour range. These drugs include Serax (oxazepam), Ativan (lorazepam), Xanax (alprazolam), and Restoril (temazepam). Temazepam has been used over the years in hospital and nursing home settings for sleep-maintenance insomnia in a 15 to 30 mg dose.[13] Using Xanax or Ativan for sleep is generally regarded as inappropriate today.

In the 1980's, the sleeping pill of choice was a short-acting benzodiazepine Halcion (triazolam). At the time, Halcion was considered a breakthrough drug because of its rapid onset of action (usually inducing sleep within 30 minutes) and short half-life (two-to-five-hour range). Unfortunately, Halcion had significant abuse potential, and was associated with early morning awakening, rebound insomnia upon abrupt withdrawal and in some patients, anterograde, or short-term amnesia. Oops. Much better options are available today.

Non-Benzodiazepine Hypnotics

It's rather odd to define something by what it is not. But that's the story with this interesting class of medications.

Also known as benzodiazepine receptor agonists (BRAs). These drugs work on benzodiazepine receptors (or GABA) in the brain, but they seem to be more selective and have fewer side effects than the older benzodiazepines.[14] Clinical experience with these medications has demonstrated less risk of tolerance, rebound insomnia, withdrawal symptoms, and addiction compared to the benzodiazepines.[15] Other clinical advantages of these agents include their ability to decrease sleep latency (you fall asleep faster) and minimal effect on sleep architecture.[16] In other words, these meds don't interfere with the deeper stages of sleep. Drugs in this class include Ambien (zolpidem), Sonata (zaleplon), and Lunesta (eszopiclone). Let's review the specifics about each one.

Ambien (zolpidem) is the most frequently prescribed sleep medication in the United States. It's also the most widely studied.[17] Ambien has a rapid onset of action, usually causing sleepiness within 30 minutes. It's important to explain this to patients. Just as people can "fight" anesthesia, sometimes insomniacs "fight" their sleep medications. You actually need to "let" it work. Don't take Ambien (or other drugs in this class) and try to do laundry, pay bills, and unload the dishwasher – 'cause you're gonna lose some dishes! Take the medication about 20 minutes before you want to go to bed. Brush your teeth, do your skin care regimen, put on some hand lotion, and go to bed. Don't take these medications on a full stomach. Fatty foods, in particular, interfere with the absorption of these drugs. Better to have a light snack (cereal, graham crackers, etc.) an hour or more before taking Ambien. Do not – repeat – do not eat half a pizza and a hot fudge sundae 10 minutes before taking Ambien. You'll be wasting an expensive medication, spending half the night with indigestion, and getting fat all at once!

Ambien represented a significant breakthrough in sleep meds because of its very short half-life of 2.5 hours. The good part is the drug is quickly cleared from the body, so you don't wake up at 6:00 am feeling like something out of "Land of the Living Dead." The bad part is Ambien will not keep you

Studies with Ambien have also shown that intermittent use can be effective in treating chronic insomnia.

asleep for seven to eight hours. Staying asleep for about 4.5 to 5 hours is more likely. Hence the introduction of Ambien CR in 2005. The controlled-release form has a mildly prolonged duration of action (and an even higher price tag).

Over the past decade some physicians have been reluctant to prescribe Ambien for more than two or three weeks. Based on research and clinical experience with the older benzodiazepine drugs, some people had concerns about rebound insomnia, tolerance, and addiction. These concerns are largely unfounded. Multiple studies on Ambien have demonstrated little or no rebound insomnia.[18,19,20] Studies with Ambien have also shown that intermittent use (three to five nights a week) can be effective in treating chronic insomnia, with continued benefit on nights the drug is taken and sleep that is no worse than baseline on nights when no Ambien is taken.[21] As an internist/geriatrician, I've had a fair amount of experience prescribing Ambien, and I have yet to see someone start taking 10 mg a night, then 20 mg, then 40 mg twice a day, then 60 mg every six hours, then start robbing 7-Elevens to get money to support her Ambien habit. That's simply not what we see in clinical practice. Some patients get to the point where they have difficulty falling asleep without Ambien. That typically reflects psychological dependence, not physiologic addiction. Remember, addiction involves requiring higher and higher doses of a substance and compulsive use despite harmful effects.

Let me add a few words about side effects and dosing. They're often related. The standard dose of Ambien is 5- or 10- mg at bedtime. However, in the elderly, 5-mg can be too much. I generally recommend 2.5-mg (breaking a 5-mg caplet in half) or taking a 10-mg caplet and cutting it in thirds with a pill-cutter. This dosing is usually well tolerated in patients who are petite or elderly (it also saves a lot of money). The most common side effects of Ambien include nausea, dizziness, and drowsiness if awakened too early. Some people have experienced vivid dreams (possibly related to REM rebound after a period of sleep deprivation). Ambien should not be used in patients with sleep apnea, severe pulmonary disease, or hepatic impairment.[22,23]

Sonata or zaleplon was approved by the Federal

Drug Administration (FDA) in August 1999 for insomnia. Sonata is chemically similar to Ambien, binding selectively to the omega-1 benzodiazepine receptor (it is not, however, a benzodiazepine). Like Ambien, Sonata decreases sleep latency and preserves sleep architecture.[24] It has the shortest half-life of any sleep med – a mere one hour. Consequently, Sonata has no significant effect on total sleep time, although it does induce sleep faster.[25] What does all of this mean in the real world? Taking Sonata at 10:00 pm is not your best bet – unless you need to get up around 3:00 am. If, however, you can fall asleep initially but find yourself wide-awake at 1:00 am, Sonata may be very helpful. As long as you can spend at least four more hours in bed, Sonata does not cause daytime drowsiness or cognitive impairment.[26] There is also no evidence of rebound insomnia after stopping Sonata.[27]

Like Ambien, Sonata has a rapid onset of action (15 to 30 minutes) and should not be taken after a fatty meal or snack. It is available in 5- or 10-mg capsules so there is not an option for tweaking the dose or breaking or cutting caplets. The pharmacodynamics of Sonata make it a useful option in elderly patients with insomnia.[28] The price tag, unfortunately, is not so great. Sonata became available as a generic in late 2008.

Lunesta (eszopiclone) is the newest non-benzodiazepine for sleep. It was approved by the FDA in 2005. Lunesta is a slightly modified version of zopiclone, a drug which has been used in Europe for over a decade. Lunesta has an intermediate half-life of six hours, so it has a longer duration of action than Ambien or Sonata. The good part is, it tends to keep people asleep longer. The bad part is, there may be some lingering morning drowsiness. One six-month study of Lunesta demonstrated a 50% reduction in sleep latency and a 65% reduction in wake time after sleep onset compared to baseline.[29] This study also showed sustained beneficial effect over six months of use without development of tolerance. As a result, Lunesta is approved by the FDA for use over a six-month period. Another randomized, double-blinded study of 231 elderly people showed that Lunesta improved sleep latency, quality, depth of sleep, and total sleep time. It also reduced nighttime awakenings as well as the number and duration of daytime naps.[30] Given these findings, Lunesta may be most helpful in patients with sleep maintenance problems, including older individuals and patients with depression. The side effect profile is similar to other drugs in this class with the added possibility of dysgeusia or an unpleasant taste for several hours. Lunesta is available in 1-, 2-, and 3- mg tablets.

In the spring of 2007, the FDA issued cautions about sleep medications causing possible allergic reactions and "complex sleep-related behaviors" such as sleepwalking, eating, or driving while not fully awake.

These problems are far more likely to be seen when patients take very large doses or combine sleep meds with alcohol or other sedating medications. Taken as directed, these drugs have been used safely for years.

Rozerem is not a CNS depressant.

Selective Melatonin Receptor Agonist

The only medication in this category (as of Fall 2008) is Rozerem (ramelteon). It was approved by the FDA in July 2005 for sleep onset insomnia. Rozerem has a unique mechanism of action, working on the suprachiasmatic nucleus as opposed to the central nervous system (CNS) globally. Since it is not a CNS depressant, it has no sedating properties and therefore no abuse potential. Rozerem is the first non-scheduled or Drug Enforcement Administration (DEA) controlled medication approved for treatment of insomnia.

Rozerem works specifically on melatonin MT1 and MT2 receptors. These receptors have specific activity. MT1 receptors promote sleep, and MT2 receptors seem to regulate the timing of circadian rhythms. In fact, Rozerem works on these receptors even more than melatonin itself. Interestingly, Rozerem does not affect GABA, histamine receptors, acetylcholine, noradrenergic receptors, or opioid receptors.[31] Physiologically speaking, that is a definite plus.

Since melatonin is a hormone, it would seem reasonable to be concerned about potential endocrine effects due to Rozerem. So far, however, the only endocrinologic effect noted has been a slight increase in prolactin levels in women.[32]

Rozerem has a half-life in the two- to five- hour range. It is metabolized in the liver, mostly through the CYPIA2 enzyme system. Translation: there is little chance of drug-drug interactions, with one significant exception, which is Luvox (fluvoxamine). Luvox is a CYPIA2 inhibitor, so combining the two drugs could cause Rozerem levels to rise. Since Rozerem is metabolized in the liver, common sense dictates it should not be used in patients with significant liver disease.

One study of chronic insomnia patients, conducted over 35 nights, demonstrated that people who received Rozerem fell asleep more quickly than those who received placebo.[33] So far, Rozerem has shown little evidence of causing withdrawal symptoms or rebound insomnia. More clinical experience will be necessary before we can know about any long-term effects. At present, Rozerem is available in an 8-mg dose.

New Drugs in the Pipeline

Several new agents are currently being studied for treatment of insomnia. The following medications are not yet approved by the FDA, but they may become available in the next few years:

★ Indiplon is a nonbenzodiazepine hypnotic that has been shown to improve sleep onset and sleep maintenance in sleep studies.[34] A sustained-release version is also under investigation.

★ Gaboxadol is the first in a novel class of sleep agents, the selective extrasynaptic gamma-amino-butyric acid-agonists, or SEGAs. These particular receptors are concentrated in areas of the brain that regulate sleep. Gaboxadol is now in phase III clinical trials. So far, it has been shown to improve sleep onset and maintenance while increasing time spent in restorative slow-wave sleep.

Also under study for insomnia are:

★ Gabitril (tiagabine), an anti-seizure drug.

★ Lyrica (pregabalin), used for seizures and neuropathic pain.

★ Neurontin (gabapentin), used for seizures

and neuropathic pain.

★ An extended-release version of Sonata (zaleplon).

And finally, in the, "Don't Even Think About It" category for sleep we have the following:

★ Antipsychotic drugs.

★ Barbiturates (Remember "Valley of the Dolls"?).

★ Chloral hydrate.

Remember – it's always best to address any problem with time-tested common sense. Begin with an understanding of what's contributing to your insomnia. Be consistent with good sleep habits. But there are times when appropriate use of sleep medications is necessary. Correcting sleep deprivation is an important way to prevent far more serious medical problems down the road.

References

1. Treatment of insomnia. *Treat Guided Med Letter*. 2006; 4: 5-10.

2. Walsh JK, Schweitzer PK. Ten year trends in the pharmacological treatment of insomnia. *Sleep*. 1999; 22: 371-375.

3. Kaynak H, Kaynak D, Gozukirmizi E, et al. The effects of trazodone on sleep in patients treated with stimulant antidepressants. *Sleep Med*. 2004; 5: 15-20.

4. Nierenberg AA, Adler LA et al. Trazodone for antidepressant-associated insomnia. *Am J Psychiatry*. 1994;151:1069-1072.

5. James SP, Mendelson WB. The use of trazodone as a hypnotic: a critical review. *J of Clinical Psychiatry*. 2004; 65: 752-755.

6. Hajak G, Rodenbeck A, Volderholzer U, et al. Doxepin in the treatment of primary insomnia: a placebo-controlled, double-blind, polysomnographic study. *J Clin Psychiatry*. 2001; 62: 453-463.

7. Asian S, Isik E, Cosar B. The effects of mirtazapine on sleep: a placebo-controlled, double-blind study in young healthy volunteers. *Sleep*. 2002; 25: 677-679.

8. Drug Facts and Comparisons. 2000. St Louis, MO.

9. Hale LS. Treating transient insomnia in older patients. *Patient Care* 2001 (March 15): 91-97.

10. Woodward M. Hypnosedatives in the elderly. A guide to appropriate use. *CNS Drugs*. 1999; 11: 263-279.

11. Ibid

12. Grunstein R. Insomnia. Diagnosis and management. *Aust Fam Physician*. 2002; 31: 1-6.

13. Shochat T, Loredo J, Ancoli-Israel S, Sleep disorders in the elderly. Curr Treat Options Neurol. 2001; 3: 19-36.

14. Harvard Mental Health Letter. 2006. Dec; 23(6). 1-5.

15. Ibid

16. Treatment of insomnia. *Treat Guided Med Letter.* 2006; 4: 5-10.

17. Ibid.

18. Walsh JK, Roth T, Randazzo A, et al. Eight weeks of non-nightly use of zolpidem for primary insomnia. *Sleep.* 2000; 23:1087-1096.

19. Soldatos CR, Dikeos DG, Whitehead A. Tolerance and rebound insomnia with rapidly eliminated hypnotics: a meta-analysis of sleep laboratory studies. *Int Clin Psychopharmacol.* 1999; 14: 287-303.

20. Scharf MB, Roth T, Vogel GW, Walsh JK. A multicenter, placebo-controlled study evaluating zolpidem in the treatment of chronic insomnia. *J Clin Psychiatry.* 1994; 55:192-199.

21. Perlis ML, McCall WV, Krystal AD, Walsh JK. Long-term, non-nightly administration of zolpidem in the treatment of patients with primary insomnia. *J Clin Psychiatry.* 2004; 65:1128-1137.

22. Holm KJ, Goa KL. Zolpidem. An update of its pharmacology, therapeutic efficacy and tolerability in the treatment of insomnia. *Drugs.* 2000; 59: 865-889.

23. Ancoli-Israel S, Richardson GS, Mangano RM. Long-term use of sedative hypnotics in older persons with insomnia. *Sleep Med.* 2005; 6: 107-113.

24. Elie R, Ruther E, Farr I, et al. Sleep latency is shortened during 4 weeks of treatment with zaleplon, a novel nonbenzodiazepine hypnotic. *J Clin Psychiatry.* 1999; 60: 536-544.

25. Walsh JK, Vogel GW, Scharf M, et al. A five week polysomnographic assessment of zaleplon 10 mg for the treatment of primary insomnia. *Sleep Med.* 2000;1: 41-49.

26. Walsh JK, Pollack CP, Scharf MB, Schweitzer PK, Vogel GW. Lack of residual sedation following middle-of-the-night zaleplon administration in sleep maintenance. *Clin Neuropharmacologicol.* 2000;23:17-21.

27. Ibid.

28. Kamel NS, Gammack JK. Insomnia in the elderly: cause, approach and treatment. *Am J Med* 2006; 119: 463-469.

29. Krystal AD, Walsh JK, Laska E, et al. Sustained efficacy of eszopiclone over 6 months of nightly treatment: results of a double-blind, placebo-controlled study in adults with chronic insomnia. *Sleep.* 2003; 26: 793-799.

30. Scharf M. Seiden D, Erman M, et al. Eszopiclone rapidly induced sleep and provided sleep maintenance in elderly patients with chronic insomnia. Chicago, IL. 11th Congress of the International Psychogeriatric Association; August 17-22, 2003.

31. Neubauer DN. Treatment of insomnia: What works – what doesn't? *Consultant.* Nov 2005; Suppl. 45. (13): 514-523.

32. Ibid.

33. Zammit G, Roth T, Erman M, et al. Polysomnography and outpatient study to determine the efficacy of ramelteon in adults with chronic insomnia. Presented at the 158th Annual Meeting of the American Psychiatric Assoc. May 21-26, 2005; Atlanta. Abstract NR613.

34. Walsh JK, Lankford DD, Krystal A, et al. Efficacy and tolerability of four doses of indiplon (NBI-34060) modified release in elderly patients with sleep maintenance insomnia. *Sleep.* 2003;26:A78.

Chapter **10**

Herbal Remedies and Other Supplements

"Adopt the pace of nature.
Her secret is patience."

—Ralph Waldo Emerson
American poet, essayist, and
philosopher (1803 - 1882)

Unfortunately, patience can be a difficult virtue under the best circumstances. And, patience can wear thin when insomnia has been dragging on for weeks or months. Prescription sleep medications can certainly offer effective and rapid relief, but they are pricey, require physician appointments and refills, and sometimes cause side effects. Many people are reluctant to take prescription hypnotics for fear of becoming dependent, a concern that has been exaggerated at times. So-called "natural" remedies may be helpful for some individuals, but caution is warranted. The word "natural" is often used rather loosely. Herbal remedies and supplements are not regulated by the Food and Drug Administration (FDA) and are often imported from other countries where "anything goes." As we'll see, "natural" does not necessarily mean "safe." Having accurate information and knowing the source of the supplement remain the best bets for safe and appropriate use.

The word "natural" is often used rather loosely.

Let's consider the major players:

Melatonin

Known to biochemists as N-acetyl-5-methoxytryptamine, melatonin is a hormone produced by the pineal gland.[1] It is a chemical precursor of serotonin, which is certainly interesting from a clinical perspective. Melatonin is rapidly metabolized (its half-life is only 45 to 50 minutes) and is taken up by tissues throughout the body. As far as we know, its primary function involves regulation of circadian rhythms. When we perceive dimming of ambient light levels, signals from the suprachiasmatic nucleus in the hypothalamus trigger increased melatonin secretion by the pineal gland. In fact, right before sleep, serum levels increase by a factor of 10 and peak somewhere between midnight and 3:00 am. Total nightly output of melatonin is higher in winter and lower in summer.[2] This is a fact that is not lost on anyone who has ever been to Alaska in January or July! As we get older, melatonin production is thought to decline but peaks much earlier in the evening. This probably explains some sleep behaviors we see in elderly patients.

Melatonin has antioxidant activity and, consequently, has been promoted for various conditions including heart disease, cancer, Alzheimer's, and general aging. Not surprisingly, since melatonin is synthesized in the same enzymatic pathway as serotonin, it has been proposed as an antidepressant. However, well-controlled, large-scale studies of the safety and efficacy of melatonin are lacking. Doses ranging from 50 micrograms (mcg) to 20 milligrams (mg) are available but the optimum dose is probably in the range of the 0.3 mg to 1.0 mg. The wide range of doses probably reflects significant variations in gastrointestinal (GI) absorption, time of administration, and type of preparation.[3] Another consideration is the fact that many melatonin studies have been conducted with normal, healthy subjects as opposed to patients with insomnia. There is some evidence that melatonin may be helpful in the setting of jet lag and adaptation to night shift work.[4]

Does melatonin really improve sleep? It depends. Melatonin has been shown to

Oh, a little Valium will help you fall asleep!

reduce sleep latency or time to sleep onset, and it decreases time to Stage 2 sleep without altering sleep architecture.[5] However, other randomized, placebo-controlled studies have not shown improvements in subjective or objective parameters.[6,7]

Melatonin is generally taken 30 minutes before bedtime. However, in the setting of delayed sleep phase syndrome, there may be greater benefit if melatonin is taken four to five hours before usual bedtime.[8]

Reliable data about the adverse effects of melatonin are limited. Dizziness, headache, fatigue, and irritability have been reported.[9] Women who are pregnant or nursing should not take melatonin, since we have no safety data.

To sum it up, melatonin may be worth a try when insomnia strikes, but a little caution is warranted. I wouldn't recommend melatonin to anyone undergoing treatment for cancer, human immunodeficiency virus (HIV), or auto-immune diseases. Pregnant women, nursing mothers, or children should not take it. Do your homework and know who the manufacturer is. A few years back, several melatonin products imported from third-world countries were found to be contaminated with benzodiazepines. Oh, a little Valium will help you fall asleep! Just be prudent.

Valerian

Valeriana officinalis is the most commonly used herbal remedy for insomnia in the United States and Europe.[10] It seems to produce sedative effects by working at gamma-amino butyric acid (GABA) receptor sites.[11] Valerian has been shown to increase slow-wave sleep.[12] Unfortunately, it has a slow onset of action (on the order of two to three weeks), so it's not particularly helpful in the acute treatment of insomnia. The most commonly used dose is 600 mg/day. Valerian can cause headaches and fatigue, but no serious adverse effects have been reported. The research literature on valerian is not of particularly good quality, since doses, preparation, and length of treatment vary considerably.[13] Given its apparent mechanism of action, I wouldn't recommend it to anyone with acute insomnia, depressive symptoms, liver disease, or migraine headaches until better research is available.

I would also caution against combining valerian

with any prescription sedatives, tranquilizers, or seizure medications.

One minor personal observation: in my opinion, valerian root bears a remarkable olfactory similarity to dirty sweat socks. When the label on a product warns of a "distinctive aroma," you know you're dealing with some pretty stinky stuff.

Chamomile

True chamomile, or *Matricaria chamomilla*, is the German variety with white flowers and yellow centers much like a daisy. Over the centuries, chamomile has been used to treat conditions as diverse as menstrual cramps, indigestion, skin irritations, colds, anxiety, and insomnia. Chamomile contains a number of flavonoids, including apigenin, which seems to have both anti-inflammatory and sedative properties.[14] Although a number of animal studies have been conducted in Europe, clinical studies in humans are limited and involve small numbers. Given centuries of use with no apparent serious problems, it's probably reasonable to try a little chamomile tea in the evening to facilitate sleep. Try steeping two tea bags in near-boiling water for five minutes about an hour before bed. (Don't drink anything too close to bedtime for the sake of your bladder.) I know of only one caution – people with allergies to plants in the daisy, aster, or ragweed families may also be allergic to chamomile. Drinking the tea or even taking capsules with chamomile can cause an irritating, itchy sensation in the mouth. That will not help anyone fall asleep!

Passion Flower

Technically known as *Passiflora incarinata*, passion flower was originally discovered in South America. It's name has nothing to do with romantic passion. Rather, its strikingly curious flower reminded Christian settlers of Christ's crown of thorns. Over the years, passion flower has been used as tinctures, teas, and in poultices for wound healing. It is believed to have calming or sedating properties, but good clinical research is lacking. Passion flower is often combined with chamomile and hops in various over-the-counter (OTC) or herbal preparations for sleep. It seems to be quite benign, but if you're already fond of Xanax (alprazolam) or Ambien (zolpidem) I doubt you'll be impressed with passion flower.

Kava-Kava

Extracted from the roots of Polynesian plant *Piper methysticum*, kava was used for centuries in the Pacific islands for medicinal and ceremonial purposes. Once it was taken back to Europe by Captain James Cook, its popularity as a "tranquilizer" increased. Kava has a rapid onset of action causing sedation.[15] Several years ago, "kava-abuse" syndrome was described. Symptoms included overuse, yellow discoloration of the skin, bilateral conjunctivitis, seizures, and hepatotoxicity. In fact, several people developed liver failure requiring transplantation.[16] It has been banned in several European countries, the United Kingdom, and in many States of the United States. Kava inhibits at least six liver enzymes, so taking it with any drug metabolized by the P450 system can cause toxicity (Valium [diazepam], Coumadin [warfarin], Haldol [haloperidol], and Prozac [fluoxetine] are examples).[17] Bottom line: Kava-kava is a big no-no!

Calcium & Magnesium

Chances are good you've already been advised to take a calcium/magnesium supplement if you're a woman. But if insomnia is a problem, the timing of your supplement may help. Calcium and magnesium work on many tissues – bones, joints, blood vessels, muscles, heart, and nervous system. If you've been instructed to take 1,500 mg of calcium per day, try this regimen: 500 mg at lunch, 500 mg at dinner, and 500 mg with a light bedtime snack. The magnesium can be dosed at 100 mg to 150 mg three times a day.

Although not clinically studied as sedatives, calcium and magnesium have been observed by some astute practitioners to have very mild, subtle calming effects. I've used and recommended this regimen for years for restless legs syndrome before dishing out heavy-duty medications.

Aromatherapy

The most studied substance in this field is lavender, which is used extensively in Europe and the United Kingdom for relaxation and sleep. Lemon balm, chamomile, and ylang

ylang are reported to induce a relaxed state conducive to sleep. So far, however, there is no evidence of a specific or direct hypnotic effect. I say it's worth a try. Why wouldn't you want your bedroom to smell nice?

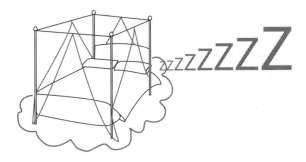

References

1. Stedman's Medical Dictionary. 27th Editions Lippincott Williams and Wilkins. Baltimore, MD. 2000; p 1084.

2. Ibid.

3. Wagner j, Wagner ML, Hening WA. Beyond benzodiazepines: alternative pharmacologic agents for the treatment of insomnia. *Ann Pharmacother.* 1998; 32: 680-691.

4. Reiter RF. Melatonin: clinical relevance. *Best Pract Res Clin Endocrinol Metab.* 2003;17: 273-285.

5. Gilbert SS, van den Heuvel CJ, Dawson D. Daytime melatonin and temazepam in young adult humans: equivalent effects on sleep latency and body temperatures. *J Physiol.* 1999;514: 905-914.

6. Ellis CM, Lemmens G, Parkes JD. Melatonin and insomnia. *J Sleep Res.* 1996; 5: 61-65.

7. James SP, Sack DA, Rosenthal NE, Mendelson WB. Melatonin administration in insomnia. *Neuropsychopharmacol.* 1990;3:19-23.

8. Budur K, Rodriguez C, Foldvary-Schaefer N. Advances in treating insomnia. *Cleveland Clinic J Med.* 2007;74: 251-266.

9. Zhdanova IV, Lynch HJ, Wurtman RJ. Melatonin: a sleep-promoting hormone. *Sleep.* 1997;20: 899-907.

10. Richman A, Witkowski JP. 5th Annual Herbal Product Sales Survey. *Whole Foods.* 1999; 22: 49-56.

11. Houghton PJ. The scientific-basis for the reputed activity of valerian. *J Pharm Pharmacology.* 1999; 51: 505-512.

12. Donath F, Quispe S, Diefenbach K, et al. Critical evaluation of the effect of valerian extract on sleep structure and sleep quality. *Pharmacopsychiatry.* 2000;33: 47-53.

13. Bent S, Padula A, Moore D, et al. Valerian for sleep: Aa systematic review and meta-analysis. *Am J Med.* 2006;119:1005-1012.

14. Roberts AJ, OBrien M, Subak-Sharpe G. *Nutraceuticals: The complete encyclopedia of supplements, herbs, vitamins and healing foods.* Penguin-Putnam, New York, NY. 2001; 414-416.

15. Wheatley D. Medicinal plants for insomnia: a review of their pharmacology, efficacy and tolerability. *J Psychopharmacol.* 2005; 19: 414-421.

16. US Food and Drug Administration, Consumer advisory. March 25, 2002. Kava-containing dietary supplements may be associated with severe liver injury. www.cfsan.fda.gov/-dms/addsdava.html.

17. Bressler R. Herb-drug interactions: interactions between kava and prescription medications. *Geriatrics.* 2005; 60:24-25.

Conclusion

Well, there you have it. Apart from air, food, and water, sleep (or the lack thereof) has the most profound impact on our well-being of any daily activity or habit. One restless, sleep-deficient night can result in a physiologic domino effect, ranging from a crabby mood to a catastrophic accident. Every organ system we have can be compromised by sleep deprivation. The good news is this: sleep has an amazing ability to restore, repair, and regenerate our worn, frazzled minds and bodies. No matter how complex and sophisticated our medical technologies become, we must never forget the healing power of sleep.

Listen to your body. Pay attention to how you feel. If you ignore the whispers of fatigue you may eventually be assaulted by the screams and shouts of exhaustion. Either way, your body will get your attention. Better to give it the rest it needs now. You could be feeling so much better in a few days.

That's pretty good advice. I think I'll heed it now. Pleasant dreams and may we all be blessed with abundant delta wave activity!